OPPOSING
VIEWPOINTS®
SERIES

Human Rights

Other Books of Related Interest

Opposing Viewpoints Series

Civil Liberties

At Issue Series

Gay Marriage

Current Controversies Series

Medicare

"Congress shall make no law … abridging the freedom of speech, or of the press."

First Amendment to the US Constitution

The basic foundation of our democracy is the First Amendment guarantee of freedom of expression. The Opposing Viewpoints Series is dedicated to the concept of this basic freedom and the idea that it is more important to practice it than to enshrine it.

Human Rights

David Haugen and Susan Musser, Book Editors

GREENHAVEN PRESS
A part of Gale, Cengage Learning

Detroit • New York • San Francisco • New Haven. Conn • Waterville. Maine • London

Elizabeth Des Chenes, *Director, Publishing Solutions*

© 2013 Greenhaven Press, a part of Gale, Cengage Learning

Gale and Greenhaven Press are registered trademarks used herein under license.

For more information, contact:
Greenhaven Press
27500 Drake Rd.
Farmington Hills, MI 48331-3535
Or you can visit our Internet site at gale.cengage.com.

For product information and technology assistance, contact us at:

Gale Customer Support, 1-800-877-4253.
For permission to use material from this text or product, submit all requests online at www.cengage.com/permissions.

Further permissions questions can be emailed to permissionrequest@cengage.com.

Articles in Greenhaven Press anthologies are often edited for length to meet page requirements. In addition, original titles of these works are changed to clearly present the main thesis and to explicitly indicate the author's opinion. Every effort is made to ensure that Greenhaven Press accurately reflects the original intent of the authors. Every effort has been made to trace the owners of copyrighted material.

Cover image © jaminwell/iStockPhoto.com.

LIBRARY OF CONGRESS CATALOGING-IN-PUBLICATION DATA

Human rights / David Haugen and Susan Musser, book editors.
    p. cm. -- (Opposing viewpoints)
    Summary: "Human Rights: Opposing Viewpoints is the leading source for libraries and classrooms in need of current-issue materials. The viewpoints are selected from a wide range of highly respected sources and publications"-- Provided by publisher.
    Includes bibliographical references and index.
    ISBN 978-0-7377-4773-7 (hardback) -- ISBN 978-0-7377-4774-4 (paperback)
    1. Human rights--Juvenile literature. I. Haugen, David M., 1969- editor of compilation.
    JC571.H76853 2013
    323--dc23
                                                                2012032614

Printed in the United States of America
1 2 3 4 5   17 16 15 14 13

Contents

Chapter 3: What Is the Impact of Religion on Human Rights?

Chapter 4: Are All Rights Human Rights?

Why Consider Opposing Viewpoints?

"The only way in which a human being can make some approach to knowing the whole of a subject is by hearing what can be said about it by persons of every variety of opinion and studying all modes in which it can be looked at by every character of mind. No wise man ever acquired his wisdom in any mode but this."

John Stuart Mill

In our media-intensive culture it is not difficult to find differing opinions. Thousands of newspapers and magazines and dozens of radio and television talk shows resound with differing points of view. The difficulty lies in deciding which opinion to agree with and which "experts" seem the most credible. The more inundated we become with differing opinions and claims, the more essential it is to hone critical reading and thinking skills to evaluate these ideas. Opposing Viewpoints books address this problem directly by presenting stimulating debates that can be used to enhance and teach these skills. The varied opinions contained in each book examine many different aspects of a single issue. While examining these conveniently edited opposing views, readers can develop critical thinking skills such as the ability to compare and contrast authors' credibility, facts, argumentation styles, use of persuasive techniques, and other stylistic tools. In short, the Opposing Viewpoints Series is an ideal way to attain the higher-level thinking and reading skills so essential in a culture of diverse and contradictory opinions.

In addition to providing a tool for critical thinking, Opposing Viewpoints books challenge readers to question their own strongly held opinions and assumptions. Most people form their opinions on the basis of upbringing, peer pressure, and personal, cultural, or professional bias. By reading carefully balanced opposing views, readers must directly confront new ideas as well as the opinions of those with whom they disagree. This is not to argue simplistically that everyone who reads opposing views will—or should—change his or her opinion. Instead, the series enhances readers' understanding of their own views by encouraging confrontation with opposing ideas. Careful examination of others' views can lead to the readers' understanding of the logical inconsistencies in their own opinions, perspective on why they hold an opinion, and the consideration of the possibility that their opinion requires further evaluation.

Evaluating Other Opinions

To ensure that this type of examination occurs, Opposing Viewpoints books present all types of opinions. Prominent spokespeople on different sides of each issue as well as well-known professionals from many disciplines challenge the reader. An additional goal of the series is to provide a forum for other, less known, or even unpopular viewpoints. The opinion of an ordinary person who has had to make the decision to cut off life support from a terminally ill relative, for example, may be just as valuable and provide just as much insight as a medical ethicist's professional opinion. The editors have two additional purposes in including these less known views. One, the editors encourage readers to respect others' opinions—even when not enhanced by professional credibility. It is only by reading or listening to and objectively evaluating others' ideas that one can determine whether they are worthy of consideration. Two, the inclusion of such viewpoints encourages the important critical thinking skill of objectively evaluating an author's credentials and bias. This evaluation will illuminate an author's reasons for taking a particular stance on an issue and will aid in readers' evaluation of the author's ideas.

It is our hope that these books will give readers a deeper understanding of the issues debated and an appreciation of the complexity of even seemingly simple issues when good and honest people disagree. This awareness is particularly important in a democratic society such as ours in which people enter into public debate to determine the common good. Those with whom one disagrees should not be regarded as enemies but rather as people whose views deserve careful examination and may shed light on one's own.

Thomas Jefferson once said that "difference of opinion leads to inquiry, and inquiry to truth." Jefferson, a broadly educated man, argued that "if a nation expects to be ignorant and free . . . it expects what never was and never will be." As individuals and as a nation, it is imperative that we consider the opinions of others and examine them with skill and discernment. The Opposing Viewpoints Series is intended to help readers achieve this goal.

David L. Bender and Bruno Leone,
Founders

Introduction

"Democracy, freedom, [and] human rights have come to have a definite meaning to the people of the world which we must not allow any nation to so change that they are made synonymous with suppression and dictatorship. . . . It is inherent in our firm attachment to democracy and freedom that we [in the United Nations] stand always ready to use the fundamental democratic procedures of honest discussion and negotiation. It is now as always our hope that despite the wide differences in approach we face in the world today, we can with mutual good faith in the principles of the United Nations Charter, arrive at a common basis of understanding."

Eleanor Roosevelt, chair of the United Nations Commission on Human Rights, September 28, 1948.

On May 19, 2012, human rights advocate Chen Guangcheng landed in the United States after a harrowing ordeal in his home country of China. Chen, a vocal critic of the Chinese government's family planning policies and treatment of women, escaped from a month-long house arrest, fled to the US embassy in Beijing, and—after some rocky negotiations between Chinese and US diplomats—was flown with his close family to

Manhattan. Many people greeted Chen upon his arrival, cheering his freedom and the cause he symbolized. According to the *Los Angeles Times*, Chen told the assembled crowd, "We should link our arms to continue in the fight for the goodness in the world and to fight against injustice."

Only a few weeks later in early June, Aung San Suu Kyi, a prodemocracy reformer in Myanmar, was allowed to leave her home country with the assurance of the military-run government that she could return. Suu Kyi lived under house arrest even before military leaders refused to recognize the results of 1990 elections that saw her National League for Democracy win 81 percent of the country's parliamentary seats. She remained a prisoner for fifteen of the twenty-one years it took for Myanmar's government to permit new elections and surprise observers everywhere with promises of greater freedoms. Suu Kyi never opted to escape her homeland for fear that she would not be allowed to return and fight for democracy. Throughout her ordeal, she became an icon to her people and to human rights activists worldwide. Her first cross-border journey in twenty-four years was to Thailand to visit with Myanmar refugees and assure them that she would take up their plight in the new parliament. During the visit, while addressing the World Economic Forum in Bangkok on June 1, Suu Kyi cautioned against "reckless optimism" in light of Myanmar's newfound openness. She told those in attendance, "Optimism is good but it should be cautious optimism. I have come across reckless optimism. A little bit of healthy skepticism is in order."

Both Chen and Suu Kyi advocate for continuing the struggle for freedom and the recognition of human rights. However, as Suu Kyi's comment makes clear, they do not expect the fight to be short-lived. Indeed, the desire for political and personal freedom has always been part of most progressive philosophies. The idea of codifying human rights, however, did not arise until after World War II and the atrocity of the Holocaust. In the wake of the war, the United Nations formed a Committee on Human

Rights to take up the task of drafting a universal charter that would enumerate the inalienable rights that all human beings possess. Put forth in 1948, the Universal Declaration of Human Rights contained thirty articles that spelled out certain guarantees such as the right to fair and public trials, the freedom from arbitrary arrest and detention, the right to freedom of thought and worship, the right to education, and the basic right to life and liberty. Forty-eight of the fifty-six countries that were part of the UN General Assembly at the time voted in favor of the declaration; the other eight countries including Saudi Arabia, South Africa, and the USSR abstained.

The Universal Declaration of Human Rights has become a blueprint for many nations that have since drafted constitutions defining and preserving the rights of their people. It has also become a springboard for other multinational agreements that proclaim recognition of human rights. Most notably, several Islamic countries insisted the UN declaration was written from a Judeo-Christian perspective that did not align well with the fundamental beliefs of Muslim holy law. In 1990, these nations came together in support of the Cairo Declaration on Human Rights in Islam, a parallel document that stipulated some of the same rights but emphasized the dominance of Muslim Shari'ah law in dictating proper punishments for crimes covered under holy mandate, reserving certain rights for men that are unavailable to women, and defining the boundaries of free expression. The UN has not endorsed this charter, claiming it places limits on the rights it guarantees. In an April 23, 2012, opinion piece for the Brookings Institution, Turan Kayaoğlu, a professor of international politics from Qatar, argued that the Cairo Declaration subverted the UN document by subordinating human rights to a religious authority. "In the modern world, Shari'ah has increasingly become integrated in states' domestic legal systems," Kayaoğlu stated. "In the absence of any international authority to decide on Shari'ah, the Cairo Declaration effectively diminishes the universality of human rights by relegating them to the discretion of governments."

As the Cairo Declaration illustrates, the United Nations has always had difficulty in supporting the right to national sovereignty and yet claiming jurisdiction over human rights violations that take an international imperative. Human rights defenders are often the first to criticize the UN for failing to compel nations to adhere stringently to the guarantees of the Universal Declaration of Human Rights. The counterargument, however, is that the United Nations must tread delicately in order to preserve global peace. Micheline Ishay, a professor of international studies at the University of Denver, suggests that maintaining this balance may not be the ideal vision for engendering a better world. In a March 1, 2010, article for *Perspectives on Global Development and Technology*, she contends that the global community—having just surpassed the sixtieth anniversary of the UN declaration—has two paths open toward the future:

> One is a dark path, already charted by the war against terror, economic recession, the rise of belligerent fundamentalism, and the impotence of international governance to prevent war and atrocities or promote human rights. . . . A second path promises to avert this dark future, by revisiting and expanding the vision of world order born out of World War II: i.e., a vision of development and nation building, a comprehensive human rights policy, and effective international governance.

The first path bespeaks the willingness of the United Nations to bow to national sovereignty in the realm of human rights protection; the second calls upon the community of nations to acknowledge the necessity of international standards.

Opposing Viewpoints: Human Rights addresses the questions at the core of Ishay's model: where do global interests and national sovereignty intersect, and which authority is paramount when they do? The chapters in this anthology ask the following questions: What Is the Status of Human Rights Worldwide?, How Should the US Government Address Human Rights Issues?, What Is the Impact of Religion on Human Rights?, and Are All

Rights Human Rights? Even as activists like Chen insist on maintaining the fight to bring "goodness in the world," getting all the diverse inhabitants of the planet to agree on what constitutes "goodness" remains a challenge. To bring peoples and nations together in support of a universal conception of rights entails sacrifice from everyone to find the reward in a shared vision of humanity.

OPPOSING
VIEWPOINTS®
SERIES

What Is the Status of Human Rights Worldwide?

Chapter Preface

According to the *Amnesty International Report 2012*, which recaps the progress of human rights on a global scale during the past year, 2011 was marked most prominently by the popular liberation movements in North Africa and the Middle East. The report states that, despite the evidence of so many people crying out for freedom, "the international community has struggled to respond effectively." Amnesty International claims that "fear, opportunity, hypocrisy and good intentions all featured in the debate" surrounding a coordinated reaction to the momentous events. The organization cites Western arms deals with autocratic regimes and the desire to not let the Middle Eastern conflagrations stir up domestic problems as reasons for a lack of collective international support for the uprisings. It was only after the uprisings appeared to be gaining ground, Amnesty said, that the West denounced the repressive measures of those in power and spoke in favor of protecting the rights of the protestors. Brian Dooley chided the United States in a March 18, 2011, column for Human Rights First by asserting, "The U.S. Government still has lots of explaining to do to the people of Egypt and Tunisia about why it supported the repressive regimes there so strongly and for so long, and needs to convince people there that it's now on the side of democracy and human rights."

The perceived lack of clarity on human rights has much to do with Western governments balancing their own economic and diplomatic interests with their avowed pledge to promote human rights. Especially in light of the events of September 11, 2001, and the subsequent war on terror, some observers have criticized the United States for trading its staunch support of human rights with a willingness to overlook certain abuses in the name of preserving national security. Writing for Al Jazeera, Shadi Mokhtari, an assistant professor at the School of International Service at American University, argues, "the most daunting legacy of

September 11th is that Americans have followed the [George W.] Bush administration's lead and gradually abandoned the notion that morally-based values such as human rights should define their identity and guide their behaviour." Mokhtari claims that the activists in Egypt, who called for autocrat Hosni Mubarak to step down from office in 2011, were far more scrupulous in demonstrating intolerance for torture and other human rights abuses than most Americans in the years following 9/11 and the invasions of Iraq and Afghanistan. In her view, the state of human rights progress may be better measured by the actions of people throwing off the shackles of repression than by the ambiguous relationship between word and deed that seems to characterize the policies of the United States and its Western allies.

In the following chapter, authors discuss the status of human rights and the challenges facing the international community in the twenty-first century.

> *"Human rights are given without having to acquire membership in a particular economic, social or political group."*

Human Rights Are Universal and Should Be Promoted in Every Country Worldwide

Dipo Djungdjungan Summa

In the following viewpoint, a scholar argues that human rights should be considered universal and observed in all societies because they protect human dignity and all cultures. He contends these rights are universal because there are no prerequisites to qualify one as deserving of them. He goes on to counter the argument that the Western origin of modern human rights makes them inapplicable in certain contexts. He maintains that their origin does not strip them of their value, nor does it mean that they unavoidably impose a Western set of values upon other cultures. Dipo Djungdjungan Summa is an Indonesian scholar who focuses on human rights observance worldwide.

As you read, consider the following questions:

1. As stated by Summa, what has been the relationship between human rights and religion throughout history?

Dipo Djungdjungan Summa, "Are Human Rights Universal?," *Peace and Conflict Monitor*, September 12, 2011. Copyright © 2011 by The University for Peace. All rights reserved. Reproduced by permission.

2. What does the author identify as some of the Western ideas that formed the basis of modern human rights?

3. How do human rights work to protect cultures, according to Summa?

What are human rights? By definition, they are entitlements exercised against the state in order to protect the human dignity of a person, precisely because of that person's humanness. The entitlements are given not because that person is a member of a particular social or political group; they are not given because of the status of his/her birth; they are given simply because of the fact that the person is a member of the human race, and as a human being he/she deserves to live a life with dignity.

Modern Human Rights Emphasize Automatic Entitlement

Throughout history and across different cultures, the concept of human dignity has been espoused. Generally, all cultures agree that human dignity should be preserved and protected. Thus, the Christians agree that all human beings are created by the image of God, and are thus subject to similar laws because they shared some common characteristic. This doctrine is rooted in an ancient Jewish belief, which is also shared by Islam. Something similar can be said for different cultural traditions; however, we need to be careful of equating all these religious and traditional notions of human dignity with the modern conception of human rights.

First, the full realization of human dignity in terms of religious belief is always tied to the concept of discrimination, which means that one will have more protection if one shares the same belief with the rulers or authorities. Different beliefs mean different protection mechanism. Although I cannot point to specific verses, whether in the Bible, Koran, or Torah, history can speak for this. Whenever a population with a certain religious belief finds itself under a ruler with another religion, the population is likely to be subjected to many discriminatory treatments, or treated as non-citizens. This is what happened to the Moslem people in the Iberian Peninsula during the re-conquest of the peninsula by the Spanish, in the fourteenth to fifteenth century—they were forced to change their religion or face punishment and discrimination. This is also what happened to Orthodox Christian populations in Asia Minor and Constantinople when that region fell to the hands of the Ottoman Turks in the fifteenth century (although, most historians in general agree that the Moslems at that time treated people from different religions better than their Christian counterparts). Therefore, even though religions recognize some universal values of human dignity that need to be protected, history has shown that in terms of practical implementation, religions (or religious rulers) treat people differently on the basis of their religion, which stands in complete opposition to the modern concept of human rights.

Second, the traditional, cultural concept of human dignity is usually attached to a series of obligations that individuals need to fulfill before their dignity is recognized. Human dignity is something that has to be earned, rather than acquired automatically simply by becoming a member of the human race. [Dean of the State University of New York at Buffalo Law School Makau W.] Mutua explains that this is how many traditional African communities view dignity. Of course, this attachment of rights to duties is not a specifically African idea. Confucianism also maintains the primacy of obligations and duties over rights, maintaining that one has certain duties toward society in accordance to one's position. The modern conception of human rights, on the other hand, recognizes only the duty of the states in protecting the human dignity of individuals, and this protection should be given without any condition attached to everyone.

Therefore, it is clear that traditional concepts of human dignity cannot be equated with the modern conception of human dignity, which are human rights. Human rights are given without having to acquire membership in a particular economic, social or political group, and it is also given without having to fulfill certain obligations and duties. It is given simply because of the fact that the beneficiary is a human being. This conception of automatic entitlement is what sets it apart.

The Ideology of Human Rights Originated in the West

Having recognized the difference between the traditional and the modern conception of human dignity, let us turn our attention to the question of origin. How did human rights come about?

It is not possible to answer the question in this short article. Human rights [had] a very long history before it was finally crystallized in the Universal Declaration of Human Rights and the subsequent treaties and covenants. One can point to many different ideas, such as the idea of natural rights which is rooted in ancient Greek Philosophy, and further propounded by Christianity. The American Declaration of Independence and the Declaration on the Rights of Men and the Citizens from the French Revolution also mentions about the "Rights of Man", although in a relatively limited way as compared to our modern understanding of human rights. There were also various suffrage movements, such as the women's suffrage movement in the nineteenth century onwards, the fight against slavery, and also the Labor movements. Before these suffrage movements, certain rights could only be enjoyed by the elites, such as the right to vote or to be elected to public offices. These suffrage movements, however, expanded the subjects of the rights recipients or the beneficiaries, giving, for example, women the right to vote, workers the right to form unions, and everyone regardless of their skin color to be free from bondage and slavery.

All those developments contribute to the development of human rights ideas as we understand it today. However, it is relevant to the current topic being discussed to note that all these things happened in the Western cultural context. In other words: the ideology of human rights as we know it today began in the West.

These things then beg the question: are human rights universal? If they came from the West, should other cultures implement human rights ideas in their respective societies?

The way I see it, rather than addressing the first question directly, it is better to re-frame it into another question: should human rights be universal? By re-framing the question, we shift the discussion from the question of origin to a question of merits, and that for me is more useful and practical rather than discussing about origins. After all, the question of origin has pretty much been settled. Also, the question of merits will very much relate to the next question on implementation.

When we talk about the merits of human rights, it should involve at least two things. The first one is whether human rights are useful in the protection of human dignity in a modern context. The second one is the relationship between human rights and non-western cultural contexts.

Modern Nation States and Citizens Benefit from Human Rights

First, about the usefulness of human rights in a modern context, I would say that human rights are useful in the context of how modern nation states are formed. This is especially true when we see that most modern nation-states do not necessarily consist of just 'one nation', or 'one religion', or even 'one culture'. In reality, especially those states that have emerged from centuries of colonialism, their borders were defined by colonial powers and these borders do not conform to the older established borders of ethnic groups and tribes. This has forced various people of different ethnicity, cultural backgrounds and religious beliefs to live together next to each other. In these countries, the principle of non-discrimination on the protection of human dignity is supremely important to bring people together into one state. This principle is what differentiates human rights from other con-

Early Human Rights Depended on National Borders

The concept of rights, including natural rights, stretches back centuries, and "the rights of man" were a centerpiece of the age of democratic revolution. But those *droits de l'homme et du citoyen* meant something different from today's "human rights." For most of modern history, rights have been part and parcel of battles over the meanings and entitlements of citizenship, and therefore have been dependent on national borders for their pursuit, achievement and protection. In the beginning, they were typically invoked by a people to found a nation-state of their own, not to police someone else's. They were a justification for state sovereignty, not a source of appeal to some authority—like international law—outside and above it.

Samuel Moyn, "Human Rights in History,"
Nation, *August 30, 2010.*

ceptions of human dignity. In this context, I would say that human rights are very useful because they provide the principle of non-discrimination.

Human rights are also useful in the context of the relations between individuals and modern nation states, especially because they center on the well-being of the individual and limit the power of the state. This limitation of state power is supremely important, especially in modern era when the exercise of state power can be very abusive towards individuals. The older and more traditional forms of political community, before the modern-nation state, recognized older forms of protection of human dignity. However, due to the modern form of the multicultural nation state, the older human dignity concepts have became obsolete, thus making modern nation-state to be potentially very abusive. Thus, the protection given by the recognition of human rights becomes a very important limitation to the power of the state. It recognizes only the obligation on the part of the state to provide for the protection, while the individuals are not required to do anything to enjoy their human rights.

Non-Western Cultures Struggle with Human Rights

Having established that, we should proceed to examine the relations between human rights and non-western cultures. Some people say that the relation is destructive. Human rights have the potential to threaten and dismantle non-western culture, because of the incompatibility of values between human rights norms and some of the traditional values of non-western societies. This argument was particularly advanced by proponents of Asian values. This is what [international studies professor] Jack Donelly tries to explain in his article "Human Rights and Asian Values: A Defense of 'Western' Universalism":

> Traditional Chinese society was dominated by the pursuit of harmony (*he*) at all levels, from the cosmic to the personal. The path to harmony was *li*. Although often translated as "propriety", that term, in contemporary American English at least, is far too weak to encompass *li*'s force, range, or depth. *Li* prescribes a complex set of interlocking, hierarchical social roles and relations centered on filial piety (*xiao* and loyalty *zhong*). Deference and mutual accommodation were the ideal. Personal ethic emphasizes self-cultivation in the pursuit of *ren* (humanness), achieved by self mastery under the guidance of *li*.
>
> This system of values and social relations is incompatible with the vision of equal and autonomous individuals that underlies international human rights norms. In fact, the "western" emphasis on individual rights is likely to seem little short

of moral inversion. Asian critics of demands for "western" (internationally recognized) human rights argue that they have developed alternative political ideals and practices that aim to preserve traditional values of family, community, decorum and devotion to duty.

In the quoted paragraph above, critics from the Asian values perspective view human rights as a "little short of moral inversion", this means that human rights threaten the moral foundation of the Asian communities. Implicit on that statement is the rejection of human rights as a value to be implemented in Asian societies because of its incompatibility with the traditional values of Asian people.

However, [economics and philosophy professor] Amartya Sen writes that the "Asian values" that some people are championing are very much contestable. Drawing from the writings and practices of various Asian philosophers and kings from different cultural and religious backgrounds, he finds that "many of these historical leaders in Asia, not only emphasized the importance of freedom and tolerance; they also had clear theories as to why this was the appropriate thing to do". He goes on to ask as to why the current leaders of Asia choose to represent Asian values as emphasizing more on the need for harmony and order, rather than describing Asian values as emphasizing on freedom and tolerance. Why choose some values over the others, sidelining values which may have some parallels and similarities with the modern conception of human rights? The answer is that "Asian values" are used by some governments to justify their own authoritarianism; that it is less a defense of traditionalism and culture than a defense of a political system.

Human Rights Protect Culture

I think, rather than viewing the relations between human rights and cultures as something that is destructive, we can actually view human rights as protecting cultures. The implementation of human rights protection empowers the people to define their own culture as they see fit, rather than something that is defined from above, by the rulers. The proposition of Asian values by some Asian governments, on the other hand, can be seen as an attempt by regimes to set a standard of behavior that is in accordance to their interest. These elites tried to freeze culture by defining it according to their own liking. I think it is this freezing of culture that threatens culture, rather than the implementation of human rights norms. By saying that a certain culture has a certain characteristic which is fixed and immutable, these rulers and elites are denying the rights of the people in that culture to transform their culture into another form that they want. By giving the people human rights, the right to transform the culture—or the right of self-determination—is protected and cannot be intruded by the state, or by the interest of the regime. Jack Donelly says, "Human rights also empower people to modify or reject parts of their traditional culture". This right to modify and transform culture should be respected and not to be constrained by the interest of the elites.

Therefore, I propose that human rights should be treated as a universal value. First, because it has at least two merits that will be very important in a modern society: the principle of nondiscrimination and the ability to limit the power of the state over individuals; and second, because it does not contradict any culture. If anything, human rights actually protect culture by giving the people the choice to transform and develop their own cultures.

> "The human rights movement lost its way by considering human rights in a vacuum, as if there are absolutes everywhere."

End Human Rights Imperialism Now

Stephen Kinzer

In the following viewpoint, a former human rights activist argues that the contemporary human rights movement wrongly seeks to promote a narrowly defined set of universal human rights in every country, regardless of the unique circumstances within a particular country. The problem with this approach, he contends, stems from the fact that each country is not at the same stage of social, cultural, or political development. Thus, in each country certain rights are more important than others to ensure stability, peace, and continued growth. He identifies instances where the focus on human rights led to increases in violence and prolonged instability, and points out countries where certain human rights are denied that also enjoy relative stability. He calls on human rights activists to be aware of the historical failures and to carefully consider how and when to force countries to adopt universal human rights. Stephen Kinzer is a journalist and author who has worked as a foreign correspondent for the New York Times *and teaches journalism and international relations at Boston University.*

As you read, consider the following questions:

1. Into what two groups does Kinzer divide human rights, and what rights fall into each group?
2. According to the author, how have rebels in Darfur utilized human rights activists to further their cause?
3. Why is the current Rwandan government regime a success, according to Kinzer, as contrasted with human rights organizations' views of this regime?

For those of us who used to consider ourselves part of the human rights movement but have lost the faith, the most intriguing piece of news in 2010 was the appointment of an eminent foreign policy mandarin, James Hoge, as board chairman of Human Rights Watch.

Hoge has a huge task, and not simply because human rights violations around the world are so pervasive and egregious. Just as great a challenge is remaking the human rights movement itself. Founded by idealists who wanted to make the world a better place, it has in recent years become the vanguard of a new form of imperialism.

Want to depose the government of a poor country with resources? Want to bash Muslims? Want to build support for American military interventions around the world? Want to undermine governments that are raising their people up from poverty because they don't conform to the tastes of upper west side intellectuals? Use human rights as your excuse!

This has become the unspoken mantra of a movement that has lost its way.

Human Rights Watch is hardly the only offender. There are a host of others, ranging from Amnesty International and Reporters Without Borders to the Carr Centre for Human Rights at Harvard and the pitifully misled "anti-genocide" movement.

All promote an absolutist view of human rights permeated by modern western ideas that westerners mistakenly call "universal". In some cases, their work, far from saving lives, actually causes more death, more repression, more brutality and an absolute weakening of human rights.

Yet, because of its global reach, now extended by an amazing gift of $100m from George Soros—which Hoge had a large part in arranging—Human Rights Watch sets a global standard. In its early days, emerging from the human rights clauses in the 1975 Helsinki Accords, it was the receptacle of the world's innocent but urgent goal of basic rights for all. Just as Human Rights Watch led the human rights community as it arose, it is now the poster child for a movement that has become a spear-carrier for the "exceptionalist" belief that the west has a providential right to intervene wherever in the world it wishes.

For many years as a foreign correspondent, I not only worked alongside human rights advocates, but considered myself one of them. To defend the rights of those who have none was the reason I became a journalist in the first place. Now, I see the human rights movement as opposing human rights.

The problem is its narrow, egocentric definition of what human rights are.

Those who have traditionally run Human Rights Watch and other western-based groups that pursue comparable goals come from societies where crucial group rights—the right not to be murdered on the street, the right not to be raped by soldiers, the right to go to school, the right to clean water, the right not to starve—have long since been guaranteed. In their societies, it makes sense to defend secondary rights, like the right to form a radical newspaper or an extremist political party. But in many countries, there is a stark choice between one set of rights and the other. Human rights groups, bathed in the light of self-admiration and cultural superiority, too often make the wrong choice.

The actions of human rights do-gooders is craziest in Darfur, where they show themselves not only dangerously naive but also unwilling to learn lessons from their past misjudgments. By their well-intentioned activism, they have given murderous rebel militias—not only in Darfur but around the world—the idea that even if they have no hope of military victory, they can mobilise useful idiots around the world to take up their cause, and thereby win in the court of public opinion what they cannot win on the battlefield. The best way to do this is to provoke massacres by the other side, which Darfur rebels have done quite successfully and remorselessly. This mobilises well-meaning American celebrities and the human rights groups behind them. It also prolongs war and makes human rights groups accomplices to great crimes.

This is a replay of the Biafra fiasco of the late 1960s. Remember? The world was supposed to mobilise to defend Biafran rebels and prevent the genocide that Nigeria would carry out if they were defeated. Global protests prolonged the war and caused countless deaths. When the Biafrans were finally defeated, though, the predicted genocide never happened. Fewer Biafrans would have starved to death if Biafran leaders had not calculated that more starvation would stir up support from human rights advocates in faraway countries. Rebels in Darfur have learned the value of mobilising western human rights groups to prolong wars, and this lesson is working gloriously for them.

The place where I finally broke with my former human-rights comrades was Rwanda. The regime in power now is admired throughout Africa; 13 African heads of state attended President Paul Kagame's recent inauguration, as opposed to just one who came to the inauguration in neighbouring Burundi. The Rwandan regime has given more people a greater chance to break out of extreme poverty than almost any regime in modern African history—and this after a horrific slaughter in 1994 from which many outsiders assumed Rwanda would never recover. It is also a regime that forbids ethnic speech, ethnically-based political parties and ethnically-divisive news media—and uses these restrictions to enforce its permanence in power.

Human Rights Depend on Local Social Contexts

In order for human rights to be implemented and to be effective instruments for social change they have to be conceptually related to local social contexts. The universalism of human rights has to be translated into local terms. This translation of universal values to local settings of power and meaning is, of course, a complex social process. While human rights are based on the idea of the universality of the conditions of human nature, local settings often have more specific meanings and problems to deal with. And this is not only a question of cultural relativism. Debates on the adequate picture of social empirical reality also occur within so-called ethical communities. . . . When a universal right is transferred to a local setting, the right is re-interpreted and re-conceptualised in order to become relevant and meaningful for the context in which people are living their lives. So what is a universal human right to life? It depends on the social context where the right is being re-interpreted and re-implemented.

Ulf Johansson Dahre, "There Are No Such Things as Universal Human Rights—On the Predicament of Indigenous Peoples, For Example," International Journal of Human Rights, *September 2010.*

By my standards, this authoritarian regime is the best thing that has happened to Rwanda since colonialists arrived a century ago. My own experience tells me that people in Rwanda are happy with it, thrilled at their future prospects, and not angry that there is not a wide enough range of newspapers or political parties. Human Rights Watch, however, portrays the Rwandan regime as brutally oppressive. Giving people jobs, electricity, and above all security is not considered a human rights achievement; limiting political speech and arresting violators is considered unpardonable.

Human Rights Watch wants Rwandans to be able to speak freely about their ethnic hatreds, and to allow political parties connected with the defeated genocide army to campaign freely for power. It has come to this: all that is necessary for another genocide to happen in Rwanda is for the Rwandan government to follow the path recommended by Human Rights Watch.

This is why the appointment of James Hoge, who took office in October, is so potentially important. The human rights movement lost its way by considering human rights in a vacuum, as if there are absolutes everywhere and white people in New York are best-equipped to decide what they are.

Hoge, however, comes to his new job after nearly two decades as editor of *Foreign Affairs* magazine. He sees the world from a broad perspective, while the movement of which he is now a leader sees it narrowly. Human rights need to be considered in a political context. The question should not be whether a particular leader or regime violates western-conceived standards of human rights. Instead, it should be whether a leader or regime, in totality, is making life better or worse for ordinary people.

When the global human rights movement emerged nearly half a century ago, no one could have imagined that it would one day be scorned as an enemy of human rights. Today, this movement desperately needs a period of reflection, deep self-examination and renewal. The ever-insightful historian Barbara Tuchman had it exactly right when she wrote a sentence that could be the motto of a chastened and reformed Human Rights Watch:

> Humanity may have common ground, but needs and aspirations vary according to circumstances.

> "Over the past two years, China has conscientiously fulfilled its obligations under the international human rights conventions to which it is a signatory."

China Is Making Significant Progress Toward Improving Human Rights

Li Guowen

In the following viewpoint, a Chinese journalist explains the progress China has made in protecting and ensuring the fundamental human rights of its citizens. According to the author, the Chinese government has inaugurated a National Human Rights Action Plan that has strengthened China's welfare commitments and guaranteed several political and civil rights. He contends that his nation is championing the right to education for millions of poor rural Chinese, granting rural areas more representation in the People's Congress, and enhancing opportunities for women to become more active in state and local affairs. Li Guowen is a writer for China Today, *an international news magazine.*

As you read, consider the following questions:

1. By the end of 2010, how many elderly Chinese were covered by old-age insurance, according to the author?

Li Guowen, "New Developments in China's Human Rights," *China Today*, vol. 60, no. 9, September 2011, pp. 44–46. Copyright © 2011 by China Today. All rights reserved. Reproduced by permission.

2. As Guowen explains, what did Amendment VIII to the Criminal Law achieve?

3. What conclusion did the 2011 UN Committee on the Elimination of Racial Discrimination reach on China's progress in this field, according to Guowen?

In April 2009 the Chinese government published the National Human Rights Action Plan of China (2009–2010), the first national plan with human rights as its theme, promoting this aspect of social and legal development. By the end of 2010, all measures stipulated in the Action Plan had been put into practice, with all the goals achieved and tasks fulfilled in the time allotted.

During the last two years, China's GDP [gross domestic product] registered an average annual growth of 9.77 percent. In 2010 the disposable income of China's urban residents increased by 11.3 percent over the previous year, a real increase of 7.8 percent after adjusting for inflation; while the net income of rural residents increased by 14.9 percent, a real increase of 10.9 percent after adjusting for inflation.

In 2009 and 2010 an additional 22.7 million urban workers found employment in this period. By the end of 2010, the official unemployment rate was 4.1 percent, 0.2 percentage points lower than the previous year, and this was the best showing since the 2008 financial crisis. The poverty-stricken of rural areas decreased to 26.88 million, a drop of 13.19 million people from 2008. The production and living conditions in the countryside saw a remarkable improvement.

Welfare and Education Benefits Have Improved

The social security system covering urban and rural areas has been improved. By the end of 2010, the population covered by basic old-age insurance increased by 38 million more people than registered two years ago, to 250 million. By the end of 2010, the basic medical insurance for urban workers and basic medical insurance for urban residents covered 430 million people while the new rural cooperative medical insurance covered over 836 million; the total number of participants reached 1.26 billion, accounting for over 90 percent of the national population. A medical insurance network covering all citizens has taken shape.

The right to an education has been bolstered. In 2010, the state exempted 130 million rural students in compulsory education from paying tuition and miscellaneous fees, and supplied them with free textbooks, and about 12.24 million boarders from poor rural families have been subsidized. By the end of 2010, 100 percent of the national population had access to nine years of compulsory education. The net enrollment rate of school-age children in elementary schools reached 99.7 percent, and the gross enrollment rate in junior high schools reached 100 percent. The illiteracy rate among the population above 15 years of age dropped to 4.08 percent.

In the three years' reconstruction since the devastating Wenchuan Earthquake, the basic living conditions of earthquake victims and the development level of the quake-hit areas have reached or surpassed pre-disaster levels. Now housing and employment for every family are guaranteed. Reconstruction in the areas hit by the Yushu Earthquake and Zhouqu mud-rock flow is advancing smoothly, and the basic human rights of residents in these areas are effectively guaranteed.

Electoral and Legislative Developments

Civil and political rights have more effective guarantees. In March 2010 the National People's Congress revised the Election Law to stipulate that deputies to the people's congresses should be elected in the same proportion as populations of urban and rural areas. The revisions broadened the representation of the people's congresses, and improved the regulations concerning election organs and procedures, better demonstrating equality among all people, regions and ethnic groups. During these two years, the state promulgated Amendment VIII to the Criminal Law, the Social Security Law, and the Tort Law, and revised the Labor, Education and Agricultural laws, and the Law on Maternal and Infant Health Care. Amendment VIII to the Criminal Law abolished the death penalty for 13 types of economic and non-violent crimes, which accounted for nearly one fifth of the total number of death penalty crimes. The amended Criminal Law restricts the application of the death penalty to people 75 years old and above. By the end of 2010, China had enacted 236 laws, 690 administrative regulations, and 8,600 local statutes. A socialist legal system with Chinese characteristics has taken shape. All aspects of the nation are guided by law, such as the economy, politics, culture, social life, and human rights.

Safeguarding Minority, Women's, and Children's Rights

Over the past two years, the state has appropriated RMB [renminbi, China's currency] 2.779 billion as a development fund for ethnic minorities. Ethnic minorities' traditions of religious beliefs and their heritage of religious culture are further protected. A bilingual teaching mode has taken shape, adapting to the language environment and educational conditions of each ethnic group.

The level of women's participation in the management of state and social affairs has been enhanced. The state has worked out and improved a set of laws and regulations concerning women's rights and interests, such as the Social Security Law, Regulations Concerning the Labor Protection of Female Staff and Workers. The National People's Congress [NPC] has conducted inspections on the enforcement of the Law on the Protection of Rights and Interests of Women, and trade unions at various levels provide legal assistance to female staff and workers.

Children's legitimate rights and interests have been safeguarded. By the end of 2010, of all the country's provinces, autonomous regions, and municipalities directly under the central government, 18 had revised the relevant local regulations in support of the Law on the Protection of Minors, and five had made local regulations to prevent juvenile delinquency. Children's rights to education and health have been effectively guaranteed. Welfare institutions for children have been established in cities at and above the prefecture level all over the country, forming a service network to ensure the welfare of children.

The state revised the Law on the Protection of Rights and Interests of the Aged, and worked out national standards including Safety Management Standards for Social Welfare Institutions. It also carries out inspections all over the nation on implementation of these standards. In 2011, the pension for retirees from enterprises was increased by RMB 140 per month on the basis of continuous increases between 2005 and 2009. China has built a number of old-age care institutions of different types.

The building of the social security systems for people with disabilities has been further strengthened. The NPC Standing Committee has placed a Mental Health Law on its upcoming lawmaking agenda. In 2010 a total of 3,592 legal aid agencies throughout the country provided legal services (e.g. defending cases in court or serving as procurators) to over 54,000 people with disabilities.

Advancing Rights Education and Supporting International Rights Conventions

At present, there are nearly 30 human rights research centers in China, set up by colleges and research institutes. Dozens of colleges are offering courses in human rights law and human rights education. Nankai University, Shandong University, and China University of Political Science and Law are among the universities that have enrolled Masters and Ph.D. candidates in human rights. The Ministry of Education has also established national-level human rights education and training bases at Nankai

China's Minister of the State Council Information Office Says China Is Committed to International Human Rights Agreements

The Chinese government has placed a high priority on international exchanges and cooperation with regard to human rights. It is willing to learn from others' strengths to offset its own weaknesses on the basis of full equality and mutual respect while participating fully in global efforts to advance the sound development of international human rights. The Chinese government has put a premium on the active role that the [United Nations] Universal Declaration of Human Rights has played in prompting the development of human rights across the globe. It also places great importance on cooperation, and fully acknowledges the aims expressed in the declaration.

Wang Chen, speech at Fourth Beijing
Forum on Human Rights, September 21, 2011.
www.china.org.cn.

University, China University of Political Science and Law, and Guangzhou University.

Over the past two years, China has conscientiously fulfilled its obligations under the international human rights conventions to which it is a signatory, and completed its second report on implementing the International Covenant on Economic, Social and Cultural Rights, its third and fourth combined report on implementing the Convention on the Rights of the Child (including its latest report on implementing the Optional Protocol on the

Sale of Children, Child Prostitution and Child Pornography), the first report on implementing the Optional Protocol on the Involvement of Children in Armed Conflict and its first report on implementing the Convention on the Rights of Persons with Disabilities. All have been submitted to the United Nations.

The Chinese government sent a delegation to a meeting held by the UN Committee on the Elimination of Racial Discrimination to discuss China's 10th, 11th, 12th and 13th combined report on its implementation of the International Convention on the Elimination of All Forms of Racial Discrimination, and held a constructive dialogue with the committee. On August 28, the committee passed and published its conclusions, which confirmed China's measures and achievements in developing the economy in the areas inhabited by ethnic minorities, supporting less-populated ethnic groups and protecting ethnic-minority cultures. The Chinese government took the committee's conclusions very seriously, and presented its own feedback materials and suggestions for the concluding report to the committee in August 2010.

Meeting International Obligations

The Chinese government has made an earnest response to the requirements of the UN Convention Against Corruption (UNCAC), and cooperates fully in international actions in this field. Since 2009 it has sent delegations to attend the Third Conference of the States Parties (CoSP) of the UNCAC, as well as all meetings and exchanges held as part of a review of the implementation of the Convention, asset recovery operations, and preventive measures taken under the framework of the Convention.

Exchanges and cooperation efforts in the field of international human rights have been vigorous. China has fulfilled the commitments set out in the Action Plan, and instigated new initiatives for the healthy development of international human rights endeavors.

China has hosted bilateral dialogues and exchanges on human rights with various countries and regional organizations, on the basis of equality and mutual respect. Consultations on human rights have been held with the EU, the US, the UK, the Netherlands, Germany and Australia, and exchanges related to human rights take place within the framework of the Asia-Pacific Region and Sub-region.

China's NGOs [non-governmental organizations] also promote cooperation and exchanges in the field of human rights. During the past two years the China Society for Human Rights Studies twice organized the Beijing Human Rights Forum, communicating with officials and experts from over 40 countries and regions and concerned international organizations.

The National Human Rights Action Plan (2012–2015) will work out new targets and concrete measures to realize them, further promoting human rights by way of expanding democracy, strengthening the legal system and improving people's livelihoods.

> "[Chinese] authorities renewed their
> commitment to strengthening the
> rule of law. However, access to justice
> remained elusive for those considered a
> political threat."

China Is Not Making Significant Progress Toward Improving Human Rights

Amnesty International

In the following viewpoint, a human rights organization finds that China has made little progress toward correcting its problematic human rights record. The viewpoint claims that China has continued to limit personal freedoms and crackdown on most forms of resistance to government rule. It has detained and persecuted dissidents and overseen communication channels in order to quash anti-government sentiment the organization says. In addition, the viewpoint states that China has waged similar campaigns against ethnic minorities to keep rebellious elements from advocating for freedom and independence. Amnesty International monitors human rights abuses worldwide.

As you read, consider the following questions:

1. What is the intent of Article 28 of China's state secrets law, as Amnesty International claims?

Amnesty International, "Annual Report: China 2011," May 28, 2011. www.amnestyusa.org.

2. What happened to Falun Gong practitioner Guo Xiaojun after being detained by Chinese authorities in January 2010 according to the viewpoint?
3. What language is being foisted upon the school systems within both the Xinjiang Uighur Autonomous Region and Tibet, according to Amnesty International?

The Chinese government responded to a burgeoning civil society by jailing and persecuting people for peacefully expressing their views, holding religious beliefs not sanctioned by the state, advocating for democratic reform and human rights, and defending the rights of others. Popular social media sites remained blocked by China's internet firewall. The authorities continued to repress Tibetan, Uighur, Mongolian and other ethnic minority populations. On the international stage, China grew more confident and more aggressive in punishing countries whose leaders spoke publicly about its human rights record.

The Underbelly of an Economic Giant

China maintained a relatively high level of economic growth compared to other major economies, despite the continuing global recession. However, it faced intensifying domestic discontent and protests stemming from growing economic and social inequalities, pervasive corruption within the judicial system, police abuses, suppression of religious freedoms and other human rights, and continuing unrest and repression in the Tibetan and Uighur regions of the country. Despite a rise in average incomes, millions had no access to health care, internal migrants continued to be treated as second-class citizens, and many children were unable to pay school fees.

The authorities renewed their commitment to strengthening the rule of law. However, access to justice remained elusive for those considered a political threat to the regime or to the interests of local officials. Political influence over and corruption within the judiciary remained endemic.

Reflecting its growing international economic and political influence, China increasingly threatened economic and political retaliation against countries that criticized its human rights record. Many countries appeared reluctant to publicly challenge China on its lack of progress on human rights, and bilateral channels, such as human rights dialogues, proved largely ineffective. The authorities reacted angrily to the news that the Nobel Peace Prize had been awarded to long-time Chinese political activist Liu Xiaobo, indefinitely postponing bilateral trade talks with Norway. Foreign diplomats reported being pressured by China not to attend the award ceremony on 10 December [2010] in Oslo.

Freedom of Expression Curtailed

The authorities stopped people from speaking out about or reporting on politically sensitive issues by accusing them of divulging "state secrets", "splittism" (ethnic minority nationalism), slander, and the crime of "subversion". Vague regulations were used to tightly control publication of politically sensitive material, including references to the 1989 Tiananmen Square demonstrations, human rights and democracy, Falun Gong [a spiritual practice banned in 1999], and Tibetan and Uighur issues. Official censorship relied heavily on "prior restraint", a form of self-censorship, and the use of an internet "firewall" that blocked or filtered out sensitive content.

The amended state secrets law, effective 10 October [2010], added a new provision, Article 28, which requires internet and other telecommunications companies to co-operate in investigations of "state secret" leaks, or face prosecution. The authorities maintained tight control over online news reports, restricting licences to large, government-backed websites. Many social media sites remained blocked, including Facebook, Twitter, YouTube and Flickr.

- On 5 July [2010], Liu Xianbin, a member of the banned Chinese Democracy Party, was detained in Suining city, Sichuan province, for "inciting subversion of state power". The charge was linked to his support for human rights activists and articles he posted on overseas websites.

- In July, Gheyret Niyaz, an ethnic Uighur, was sentenced to 15 years in prison for "leaking state secrets". Evidence used against him included essays he had written on the economic and social conditions of Uighurs in China. It was reported that his sentence was also linked to comments he made to foreign media which criticized government policies in the Xinjiang Uighur Autonomous Region (XUAR).

Crackdown on Unregistered Religions

The state required all religious groups to register with the authorities, and controlled the appointment of religious personnel. Followers of unregistered or banned religious groups risked harassment, persecution, detention and imprisonment, with some groups labelled "heretical cult organizations" by the authorities. Churches and temples constructed by religious groups deemed illegal by the state risked demolition. More than 40 Catholic bishops of unregistered "house churches" remained in detention, under house arrest, in hiding or unaccounted for.

- In December [2010], over 100 students from a Catholic seminary in Hebei province protested against the appointment of a non-Catholic government official as school head—the first protest of its kind since 2000.

- Alimjan Yimit's 15-year sentence was upheld on appeal by the XUAR People's High Court in March [2010]. Alimjan Yimit was detained for "leaking state secrets" after he spoke twice with an American Christian in Urumqi city in April and May 2007.

Persecuting the Falun Gong

The authorities renewed the campaign to "transform" Falun Gong practitioners, which required prison and detention centres to force Falun Gong inmates to renounce their beliefs. Those considered "stubborn," that is, those who refuse to sign a statement to this effect, are typically tortured until they co-operate; many die in detention or shortly after release.

Falun Gong members continued to be targeted in security sweeps carried out prior to major national events. Falun Gong sources documented 124 practitioners detained in Shanghai prior to the World Expo, with dozens reported to have been sentenced to terms of Re-education through Labour or prison. Human rights lawyers were particularly susceptible to punishment by the authorities for taking on Falun Gong cases, including losing their licences, harassment and criminal prosecution.

- Guo Xiaojun, a former lecturer at a Shanghai university and a Falun Gong practitioner, was detained in Shanghai in January [2010] and later charged with "using a heretical organization to subvert the law". He was sentenced to four years in prison for allegedly having distributed Falun Gong materials. He was tortured in detention, kept in solitary confinement and eventually signed a confession that was used to uphold his sentence at a closed appeal hearing. He had already previously served a five-year prison term for his beliefs.

- Lawyers Tang Jitian and Liu Wei had their licences permanently revoked in April by the Beijing Municipal Justice Bureau, on grounds of "disrupting the order of the court and interfering with the regular litigation process". The two had represented a Falun Gong practitioner in April 2009 in Sichuan Province.

Human Rights Defenders in Detention

Civil society continued to expand, with increased numbers of NGOs [non-governmental organizations] operating in the country. However, the authorities tightened restrictions on NGOs and human rights defenders. In May, under pressure from the authorities, Beijing University severed links with four civil society groups, including the Center for Women's Law and Legal Services.

- Prominent human rights lawyer Gao Zhisheng, who had "disappeared" while in the custody of public security officials in February 2009, remained unaccounted for after briefly resurfacing in April [2010].

- Chen Guangcheng, who was released from prison on 9 September, and his wife, remained under house arrest. They could not leave their home, even to seek medical care.

- Tian Xi, who contracted HIV and hepatitis B and C through a blood transfusion in 1996 when he was nine years old, was tried on 21 September on charges of "intentionally damaging property". For years, Tian Xi had lobbied the hospital for compensation for himself and others infected through blood transfusions there. On 2 August, he lost his temper in a meeting at the hospital and knocked some items off a desk. Through a legal loophole his trial was suspended, allowing the authorities to keep him in indefinite detention.

Injustice in Legal Prosecution

The use of illegal forms of detention expanded, including prolonged house arrest without legal grounds, detention in "black jails", "brain-washing" centres, psychiatric institutions, and unidentified "hotels". The government did not make any progress on the reform or abolition of systems of administrative detention, including Re-education through Labour, used to detain people without charge or trial. Hundreds of thousands continued to be held in such facilities.

Torture and other ill-treatment remained endemic in places of detention. Amnesty International received reports of deaths in custody, some of them caused by torture, in a variety of state institutions, including prisons and police detention centres. In July, new regulations were introduced to strengthen prohibitions against the use of illegal oral evidence in criminal cases, including coerced confessions. However, China's Criminal Procedure Law had not yet been amended to explicitly prohibit the use of confessions obtained through torture and ill-treatment as evidence before the courts.

Statistics on death sentences and executions remained classified. However, publicly available evidence suggested that China continued to use the death penalty extensively, with thousands being executed after unfair trials. A number of cases where innocent people were sentenced to death or executed became heated topics of public debate, putting pressure on the authorities to address the issue.

State Abuse in the Xinjiang Uighur Autonomous Region

The authorities failed to independently investigate the clashes of July 2009 in Urumqi city, including possible abuse of state power. People involved in the clashes continued to be sentenced after unfair trials. In March [2010], Nur Bekri, governor of the XUAR, announced that 97 cases involving 198 individuals had been tried; however, only 26 cases involving 76 individuals were made public. The authorities continued to warn human rights lawyers against taking up these cases and in January the XUAR High People's Court issued "guiding opinions" to the courts specifying how such trials should be conducted.

Security measures were tightened in the XUAR, including revision of the Comprehensive Management of Social Order, effective 1 February [2010]. This renewed the authorities' commitment to "strike hard" against crime in the region, in particular, crimes of "endangering state security". The authorities announced

A History Professor Explains How China's Economic Advantage Is Tied to the Suppression of Human Rights

Aside from the traditional advantages of low wages and low benefits, China uses the "advantage" of "low human rights" to push down the costs of the four key factors of production: labor, land, capital, and non-renewable resources. China has shown an astonishing degree of competitive power that is rarely seen in either free market states or welfare states, and has left countries that are transitioning to democracies, whether by "gradualism" or "shock treatment," far behind. China has achieved this not by not permitting bargaining, and limiting or even abolishing trading rights to "lower transaction costs," but by refusing democratization, suppressing public participation, ignoring ideas, deriding beliefs, scorning justice, and stimulating the appetite for material things in order to induce people to concentrate their energies on the impulse of the illusory single-minded pursuit of wealth.

Qin Hui, "China's Low Human Rights Advantage," China Rights Forum, *no. 1, 2009.*

that 376 such cases had been tried in 2010 in the XUAR, up from 268 in 2008.

Silencing Resistance

Freedom of expression in the XUAR was severely curtailed by laws criminalizing the use of the internet and other forms of digital communication. Infractions included vaguely defined crimes of "ethnic separatism", such as "inciting separatism", and distributing materials and literary works with "separatist content". After partial restoration of text messaging in January [2010], over 100 people were detained for "spreading harmful information" and "harming ethnic unity" by sending text messages, five of whom were taken into criminal custody. The complete block on information and communications imposed across the XUAR in the aftermath of the July 2009 unrest was almost fully lifted in May; however, several popular Uighur websites remained banned.

A "central work forum" held in May set out ambitious economic and political plans for the region, but did not address long-standing grievances of Uighurs, including serious employment discrimination. The XUAR authorities pushed forcefully ahead with the "bilingual education" policy which in practice promotes the use of Mandarin Chinese as the language of instruction while marginalizing Uighur and other ethnic minority languages, even in ethnic minority schools.

- In July, Uighur website managers Nureli, Dilixiati Perhati and Nijat Azat were sentenced to three, five and 10 years respectively in July for "endangering state security" through postings on their websites.

- On 1 April [2010], the Urumqi Intermediate People's Court sentenced Gulmira Imin, a Uighur website administrator, to life in prison for "splittism, leaking state secrets, and organizing an illegal demonstration". It was believed the charges were linked to regular postings she made to the website Salkin, which was one of the websites on which the call to join the protests on 5 July 2009 was published.

The Tibet Autonomous Region Is Under Cultural Assault

The authorities continued to crack down on local protests associated with the March 2008 protests. Leading Tibetan intellectuals were increasingly targeted, with a number of well-known people in arts, publishing and cultural circles being sentenced to harsh sentences on spurious charges. Providing information on politically sensitive topics to foreigners was severely punished. Thousands of Tibetan students demonstrated against an official language policy which imposed Mandarin Chinese as the main language of instruction in schools at the expense of Tibetan. The policy is widely seen by Tibetans as a threat to the preservation of their culture. Although the authorities did not suppress these protests, they reiterated their commitment to the policy. Demonstrations by hundreds of Tibetan students against this policy spread to the Beijing National Minorities University in October.

The authorities continued to restrict freedom of religion. The official Buddhist Association of China issued measures, effective 10 January [2010], calling for the Democratic Management Committees of monasteries and nunneries to verify the "conformity" of religious personnel with political, professional and personnel criteria, giving the authorities another way to weed out politically "unreliable" religious leaders.

- In May, Tagyal, a Tibetan intellectual who worked in a government publishing house, was charged with "inciting splittism" after he warned Tibetans to avoid corrupt official channels when donating money to victims of the April Yushu earthquake in Qinghai. Tagyal had also published a book on the 2008 Tibetan protests.

Hong Kong Special Administrative Region Sees Only Limited Reform

The government proposed amendments allowing limited reform of the methods for electing the Legislative Council (LegCo) and selecting the Chief Executive in 2012. This prompted calls for speedy progress towards universal suffrage as stipulated in the Basic Law. LegCo passed the amendments in June, only after a controversial last minute compromise between the central government and the Democratic Party. This extended a second vote to all the electorate via a functional constituency composed of district councillors.

Foreign nationals denied entry to Hong Kong included Chen Weiming, sculptor of the Goddess of Democracy statue used in the 4 June 1989 Tiananmen vigil, and six Falun Gong dance troupe technicians.

- In January, police used pepper spray to disperse thousands of demonstrators surrounding the LegCo building during voting on a HK $66.9 billion (US $8.6 billion) rail link with Guangdong province. Protesters highlighted inadequate consultation or compensation for those evicted.

- On 29 and 30 May, police arrested 13 activists and twice confiscated Goddess of Democracy statues. . . . Using new tactics, hygiene department officials pursued prosecution for failure to obtain a "public entertainment" licence. Following public criticism, the statues were returned before the Tiananmen vigil which attracted between 113,000 and 150,000 participants.

Several activists prosecuted for unlawful assembly or assaulting officers while demonstrating outside the Central Government Liaison Office were acquitted. In August, police issued internal guidelines on charging individuals for assaulting security officers after public criticism of cases perceived as frivolous prosecutions or biased sentencing.

In April [2010], the government issued administrative guidelines on promoting racial equality.

- In May, a coroner's jury returned a verdict of lawful killing over the March 2009 hillside shooting of Hong-Kong born Nepali street sleeper, Dil Bahadur Limbu, by a police constable investigating a nuisance complaint. Ethnic minority groups had called for an independent commission of inquiry. Application for judicial review by Dil Bahadur Limbu's widow was pending.

• In October a post-operative transsexual woman lost her legal challenge for the right to marry her boyfriend in her reassigned sex.

The Peril of Deportation from Hong Kong

A 2009 pilot scheme, screening applicants opposing deportation on grounds that they would be at risk of torture, completed 122 applications in 10 months, leaving a backlog of 6,700.

• In November, three UNHCR [United Nations High Commissioner for Refugees] mandated refugees and one successful torture claimant [who was a long-term resident of] Hong Kong challenged the constitutionality of policies denying them legal status, visas and the right to work.

"The passage of new laws that guarantee equal rights for women means little if those guarantees are not fully enforced by state authorities."

Middle Eastern Women Still Face Slow Progress in Overcoming Oppression

Sanja Kelly

In the following viewpoint, a researcher asserts that while women in Middle Eastern countries have made some progress toward increased representation and the acquisition of more personal freedoms, their status is still secondary to men. She contends that women are still routinely barred from certain occupations and must prove themselves to a higher standard than their male counterparts in order to be taken seriously in academia and the marketplace. Sanja Kelly is a senior researcher and managing editor at Freedom House, a non-governmental organization that monitors and promotes democracy and human rights worldwide.

As you read, consider the following questions:

1. What does Kelly mean when she refers to the "sticky floor" that young, ambitious Middle Eastern women face in the workplace?
2. What does Kelly suggest might explain why many women in the Middle East do not file domestic violence complaints?
3. According to the author, what disparity exists in Gulf Coast countries between men and women who wish to file for divorce from their spouses?

As the societies of the Middle East and North Africa (MENA) undertake the difficult process of enacting social and political change, the unequal status of women stands out as a particularly formidable obstacle. This study presents detailed reports and quantitative ratings on the state of women's rights in the member states of the Gulf Cooperation Council (GCC): Bahrain, Kuwait, Oman, Qatar, Saudi Arabia, and the United Arab Emirates (UAE). . . . Although the study indicates that a substantial deficit in women's rights persists in every country of the Gulf region and is reflected in practically every facet of their societies, its findings also include the notable progress achieved over the last five years, particularly in terms of economic and political rights.

The Gulf region, and the Middle East as a whole, is not the only region of the world where women experience inequality. In Asia, Africa, Latin America, Europe, and North America, women continue to face discrimination and significant barriers to the full realization of their rights. It is in the Gulf, however, that the gap between the rights of men and those of women has been most clear and substantial. The Gulf countries were the worst performers in nearly all subject areas examined in the 2005 Freedom House study *Women's Rights in the Middle East and North Africa: Citizenship and Justice*, scoring particularly poorly in the categories analyzing legal rights and protection from discrimination, political rights, as well as women's personal status and autonomy.

The country reports presented in this [viewpoint] detail how women throughout the Gulf continue to face systematic discrimination in both laws and social customs. Deeply entrenched societal norms, combined with conservative interpretations of Islamic law, continue to relegate women to a subordinate status. Women in the region are significantly underrepresented in senior positions in politics and the private sector, and in some countries they are completely absent from the judiciary. Perhaps most visibly, women face gender-based discrimination in personal-status laws, which regulate marriage, divorce, child custody, inheritance, and other aspects of family life. Family laws in most of the region declare that the husband is the head of the family, give the husband power over his wife's right to work and travel, and in some instances specifically require the wife to obey her husband. Domestic violence also remains a significant problem.

Modest but Important Progress

Important steps, however, have been taken in each country over the last five years to improve the status of women. In 2005, women in Kuwait received the same political rights as men, which enabled them to vote and run for office in the parliamentary elections the following year. In Bahrain and the UAE, the first women judges were appointed in 2006 and 2008, respectively, setting an important precedent for the rest of the region. Moreover, the codification of family laws in Qatar and the UAE has been seen as another step forward; previously, family issues were decided based on each judge's interpretation of Islamic law. Since 2003, women have become more visible participants in public life, education, and business in all of the Gulf countries, including Saudi Arabia. They have also gained more freedom to travel independently, as laws requiring a guardian's permission for a woman to obtain a passport have been rescinded in Bahrain and Qatar during this report's coverage period.

In Qatar and the UAE, the positive change has come as the result of an increased political will to engage on the issue of women's rights, as well as advocacy by powerful, well-connected women such as Sheikha Moza, a wife of the emir [monarch] of Qatar. In Kuwait, Bahrain, and Saudi Arabia, reform is driven in large part by the strong grassroots efforts of women's rights activists, lawyers, and journalists. An earlier push to improve the quality of women's education, combined with the growing presence of women in the workplace, has prompted an increasing number of women to demand greater rights in other spheres of life, including politics and family.

Challenges to Equality Remain

In nearly all of the countries examined, however, progress is stymied by the lack of democratic institutions, an independent judiciary, and freedom of association and assembly. In Oman, Qatar, Saudi Arabia, and the UAE, excessively restrictive rules on the formation of civil society organizations make it extremely difficult for women's advocates to effectively organize and lobby the government for expanded rights. The lack of research and data on women's status further impedes the advocacy efforts of nongovernmental organizations (NGOs) and activists. And ultimately, the passage of new laws that guarantee equal rights for women means little if those guarantees are not fully enforced by state authorities. Throughout the region, persistent patriarchal attitudes, prejudice, and the traditional leanings of male judges threaten to undermine these new legal protections.

One of the greatest challenges to women's rights in the Gulf is the issue of female migrant workers. Although they represent a large proportion of the female population in these countries, particularly in the UAE, Qatar, and Kuwait, they are often vulnerable to abuse by private employers due to language barriers, lack of education about their rights, and a lack of protection under national labor laws. In many instances, female migrant workers face slavery-like conditions when engaged in domestic employment: their freedom of movement is limited, their employers illegally confiscate their passports to prevent them from running away, and they are subjected to verbal and physical abuse. In recent years, several countries have instituted basic legal protections for domestic workers; however, it is too early to judge the effectiveness of such measures. . . .

Economic Empowerment Grows Despite Persistent Challenges

Due to their abundant natural resources, most GCC countries have experienced unprecedented growth and development of late, and are currently undergoing an economic and cultural metamorphosis. The effects of these changes on women and their rights cannot go unnoticed.

In nearly all countries, women today are better represented in the labor force and play a more prominent role in the workplace than was the case five years ago. In Kuwait, for example, the proportion of adult women with jobs has increased from 46 percent in 2003 to 51 percent in 2007. Similarly, the proportion of working women has grown by 4 percent in Oman (to 25 percent) and by 3 percent in the UAE (to 41 percent) over the same period. Compared with male employment, however, these figures remain glaringly low. Over 80 percent of working-age men in each country are employed, though those figures have remained static over the last five years.

The growing number of working women appears to be the result of increased literacy and educational opportunities, slowly changing cultural attitudes, and government policies aimed at reducing dependence on foreign labor. Although society as a whole tends to view formal employment and business as male activities, parents and husbands alike are starting to rely more on the financial support provided by their daughters and wives. In Bahrain, several women interviewed for this study said that their prospects of marriage will increase if they hold a solid job, as "young men nowadays look for a wife that can help with family expenses."

One of the main benefits women receive from a job is a degree of financial independence from families and husbands, something they lacked in the past. Divorced or widowed women increasingly seek out employment to support themselves, instead of relying on their extended families. With divorce rates in 2005 reaching 46 percent in the UAE, 38 percent in Qatar, and approximately 33 percent in Kuwait and Bahrain, women increasingly see this separate income as vital insurance against the breakup of their marriages. Whether married or not, working women say that they have started to earn greater respect and have a greater voice within their families because they are contributing financial support.

Government policies designed to reduce dependence on foreign labor in most of the Gulf have led companies to start aggressively recruiting women to fill newly established quotas for citizen employees. In the UAE, for example, the Ministry of Labor no longer allows work permits for foreigners employed as secretaries, public-relations officers, and human-resources personnel; consequently, most of the new hires for those positions are Emirati women. In Oman, a policy of "Omanization" has had a particularly positive effect on poor, less-educated women, who have been able to obtain jobs as cleaners, hospital orderlies, and kitchen help, allowing them to support themselves in the face of economic hardship and giving them a new role in the community.

Although such policies have increased the overall number of working women, they have also highlighted the cultural limits placed on female professionals. Many women complain of difficulty in advancing beyond entry-level positions despite their qualifications and job performance, leading to a popular perception that they were hired only to satisfy the government quotas. In fact, as noted in the UAE report, these policies have resulted in a "sticky floor" for young and ambitious women. Throughout the region, very few women are found in upper management and executive positions, arguably due to cultural perceptions that women are less capable, more irrational, and better suited for family responsibilities.

Women throughout the region earn less than men despite labor laws that mandate equal pay for the same type of work and equal opportunities for training and promotion. While such laws are essential, they are frequently violated in terms of salary and employment perks like housing allowances or loans for senior officials. Women in most countries can file discrimination complaints with government agencies, but such bodies often lack the capacity to investigate discrimination cases or impose penalties for violations by employers, rendering their work largely ineffective.

Several long-standing cultural mores regarding proper professions for women remain cemented into the law. In virtually every country in the region, labor laws prohibit women from undertaking dangerous or arduous work, or work which could be deemed detrimental to their health or morals. All six countries prohibit women from working at night, with the exception of those employed in medicine and certain other fields. While these provisions are seen locally as a means of protecting women, in effect they treat women as minors who are unable to make decisions regarding their own safety and hold women's guardians responsible if the rules are violated. Since most nationals opt to work in the public sector due to shorter workdays hours and better pay, these restrictions do not affect a great number of women. Nonetheless, new labor laws in the UAE, Bahrain, Kuwait, and Qatar have reaffirmed these rules during the period under examination.

Academic Opportunities Expand Women's Prospects

Education has been a prime area of progress for women in the region, and it is an important avenue for their advancement toward broader equality. Since the 1990s, women in all six Gulf countries have made gains in access to education, literacy, university enrollment, and the variety of subjects of study available to them. That trend has continued, for the most part, over the past five years. The primary school completion rate for girls has grown by 15 percent in the UAE, 12 percent in Qatar, and 3 percent in Oman. Moreover, Qatar and the UAE now have the highest female-to-male university enrollment ratio worldwide, with women outnumbering men three to one.

Although women are generally encouraged to study in traditionally female disciplines such as education and health care, they have started entering new fields, including engineering and science. For example, in Qatar, women were accepted for the first time in 2008 in the fields of architecture and electrical and chemical engineering. In Saudi Arabia, three educational institutions started to permit women to study law in 2007, although they are only allowed to act as legal consultants to other women and remain prohibited from serving as judges and lawyers in court.

Despite these improvements, there are still many barriers to true gender equality in education. In Kuwait and Oman, women are required to achieve higher grade-point averages (GPAs) to enroll to certain disciplines at the university level. For example, female students in Kuwait must obtain a 3.3 GPA to be admitted to the engineering department, while male students need only a 2.8 GPA. As women comprise almost two-thirds of the student body at Kuwait University, the disparity in admission requirements is explained by university officials as "reverse discrimination," intended to increase the percentage of male students in certain academic fields. Moreover, in most countries examined, universities largely remain segregated by gender. It is unclear to what extent the segregation affects the quality of education, but in at least some countries, including Saudi Arabia, the number and diversity of classes offered to men are much greater than those available to women.

Protection from Domestic Violence Remains Minimal

While no part of the world is free from the stain of domestic abuse, the Gulf countries, and the MENA region as a whole, are exceptional in their array of laws, practices, and customs that pose major obstacles to the protection of women and the punishment of abusers. Physical abuse is generally prohibited, but no country in the Gulf region offers specific protections against domestic violence or spousal rape. Other factors include a lack of government accountability, a lack of official protection of rights inside the home, and social stigmas that pertain to female victims rather than the perpetrators.

No comprehensive studies on the nature and extent of domestic violence have been conducted in the Gulf states, apart from Bahrain. Nevertheless, domestic abuse is thought to be widespread in every country in the region, with its existence typically covered up by and kept within the family. Many women feel that they cannot discuss their personal situation without damaging their family honor and their own reputation. Consequently, abused women rarely attempt to file complaints with the police. When they do choose to seek police protection, they frequently encounter officers who are reluctant to get involved in what is perceived as a family matter and who encourage reconciliation rather than legal action. In Saudi Arabia in particular, guardianship laws make it very difficult for battered wives to find a safe haven. For example, this study cites the case of a girl who sought police protection after being sexually molested by her father, only to be turned away and told to bring her father in to file the complaint.

Over the last five years, several countries have taken limited steps to combat domestic violence. In the UAE, the first government-sponsored shelter for victims of domestic violence opened in Dubai in 2007 under the auspices of the Dubai Foundation for Women and Children. The shelter has a residential capacity, offers legal assistance for the victims, and provides training for the police on how to handle domestic violence cases. While this is a sign of progress, as it indicates an official acknowledgment that the problem exists, a single shelter is grossly inadequate for the needs of the emirate and the entire country.

Islamic Women Face a High Degree of Human Rights Abuses

Female genital mutilation, daughter- and wife-beating, child and arranged marriage, polygamy, *purdah* [veiling], easy divorce for men, female sexual and domestic slavery, veiling, routine rape and gang-rape and honor killing—none of these are unique to Islam.

But no other ideology, religious or otherwise, sanctions and excuses them all in the way that Islam does. Women in Islamic societies suffer on a daily basis from these indignities, violations of their human rights, and acts of violence. Some of these human rights abuses are prosecuted in the West, although advocates of "multiculturalism" argue for their acceptance. In the Arab and Islamist-jihadic world these abuses are considered "normal" and justifiable "cultural" expressions of identity. Moreover, they are connected to the terrorist mentality. As [US author and former philosophy professor] Christina Hoff Sommers has written, "After all, the oppression of women is not an incidental feature of the societies that foster terrorism. It is a linchpin of the system of social control that *jihadists* are fighting to impose worldwide."

> *Robert Spencer and Phyllis Chesler,* The Violent Oppression of Women in Islam. *Los Angeles: David Horowitz Freedom Center, 2007.*

In Bahrain, the number of NGOs that support victims of domestic violence is steadily increasing, and a growing number of women seem to be aware of such organizations and the services they provide. Several new shelters have opened over the last five years, and civil society has become more active in its advocacy efforts. The issue of domestic violence has also garnered more attention in Qatar and Saudi Arabia, although it is unclear what practical steps those governments intend to take to combat the problem. In Kuwait, there is not one shelter or support center for victims of domestic abuse.

Political Rights Rise amid Low Regional Standards

Throughout the Gulf, both male and female citizens lack the power to change their government democratically and have only limited rights to peaceful assembly and freedom of speech. According to *Freedom in the World*, the global assessment of political rights and civil liberties issued annually by Freedom House, none of the GCC countries earn the rating of "Free," and none qualify as electoral democracies.

Despite the overall lack of freedom, however, women have made notable gains over the last five years in their ability to vote and run for elected offices, hold high-level government positions, and lobby the government for expanded rights. These reforms have been most visible in Kuwait, where women received the same political rights as men in 2005 and exercised those rights for the first time in the parliamentary elections of 2006. Although none of the 27 female candidates who ran that year were successful, several came close, and women's chances are expected to improve as they receive more training and acquire experience in campaigning and electoral politics.

In the UAE, eight women were appointed and one secured election to the 40-member Federal National Council (FNC), an advisory body to the hereditary rulers of the seven emirates. Previously, no women had served on the FNC, which until 2006 was fully appointed by the seven rulers in a number proportionate to each emirate's population. In other countries, such as Oman and Bahrain, the government has appointed an increasing number of women to unelected positions, including cabinet and diplomatic posts. In addition to serving in the executive and legislative branches of government, women in the UAE and Bahrain are now permitted to act as judges and prosecutors. Although women remain severely underrepresented in political and leadership roles, their increased visibility in public life could help to change cultures in which only men are seen as leaders and decision-makers.

Working from outside the government, women's advocates in several countries have been able to lobby for expanded rights more effectively in recent years, despite persistent restrictions on freedom of association. This has been particularly evident in Kuwait, where activists played the central role in urging the government to provide women with equal political rights. In Saudi Arabia, a growing number of journalists and advocates are slowly pushing back societal boundaries and demanding increased rights. For example, in 2007 the Committee for Women's Right to Drive organized a petition addressed to the king, which prompted the government to reevaluate its ban on female drivers and announce in 2008 that women would be allowed to drive within a year. However, throughout the region, restrictions on civic organizations represent one of the main impediments to the expansion of women's rights, since activists are unable to organize and voice their demands without fear of persecution.

Legal Discrimination Remains an Obstacle

In 2004, Qatar joined Oman and Bahrain in adopting a legal provision specifying that there shall be no discrimination on the basis of sex. While the constitutions of Kuwait and the UAE do not include a gender-based nondiscrimination clause, they do declare that "all citizens are equal under the law." Only in Saudi Arabia does the constitution lack a provision committing the government to a policy of nondiscrimination.

Regardless of constitutional guarantees, women throughout the region face legal forms of discrimination that are systematic and pervade every aspect of life. For example, in none of the Gulf countries do women enjoy the same citizenship and nationality rights as men, which can carry serious consequences for the choice of a marriage partner. Under such laws, a man can marry a foreign woman with the knowledge that his spouse can become a citizen and receive the associated benefits. By contrast, a woman who marries a foreigner cannot pass her citizenship to her spouse or her children. Children from such marriages must acquire special residency permits, renewable annually, in order to attend public school, qualify for university scholarships, and find employment.

Over the last five years, a few countries have made it possible, in very limited circumstances, for foreign husbands and children of female citizens to obtain citizenship. In Saudi Arabia, amendments to the citizenship law in 2007 allowed the sons of citizen mothers and noncitizen fathers to apply for Saudi citizenship once they turn 18, but similarly situated daughters can obtain citizenship only through marriage to a Saudi man. In Bahrain, over 370 children of Bahraini mothers and noncitizen fathers were granted Bahraini citizenship in 2006, but this was an ad hoc decision made at the discretion of the king, and there is no guarantee that it will be repeated in the future. While some of these measures technically represent modest improvements, the vast extent of gender discrimination in citizenship rights remains largely unchanged.

Women's rights organizations, particularly in Bahrain and Kuwait, have taken up citizenship inequality as one of their main causes and have actively lobbied their governments for reform. However, many in the region believe that if these laws were changed, foreign men would easily "trick and seduce" national women in order to obtain citizenship and receive the substantial social benefits that it confers.

Apart from citizenship, women also face gender-based restrictions in labor laws, can legally be denied employment in certain occupations, and are discriminated against in labor benefits and pension laws. However, gender inequality is most evident in personal-status codes, which relegate women to an inferior position within marriage and the family, declare the husband to be the head of household, and in many cases require the wife to obey her husband. Under the family codes of all six Gulf countries, a husband is allowed to divorce his wife at any time without a stated reason, but a wife seeking divorce must either meet very specific and onerous conditions or return her dowry through a practice known as *khula*. Furthermore, women need a guardian's signature or presence in order to complete marriage proceedings, limiting their free choice of a marriage partner. In Bahrain and Saudi Arabia, there is no codified personal-status law, allowing judges to make decisions regarding family matters based on their own interpretations of Islamic law.

Women's rights organizations in Bahrain have been advocating for codified personal-status laws for close to two decades. A draft law was introduced in the parliament in December 2008 and is currently being reviewed by the relevant officials; the strongest opposition to its adoption comes from conservative Shiite Muslim groups. In the UAE and Qatar, the personal-status laws were codified for the first time in 2005 and 2006, respectively. Although the new laws contain certain provisions granting women additional rights and are viewed as a positive development, many clauses simply codify preexisting inequalities.

Several other legal changes over the last five years, if properly implemented, have the potential to improve women's rights. For example, laws requiring women to obtain permission from their guardians in order to travel were rescinded in Bahrain and Qatar. In Oman, the government introduced a law in 2008 stipulating that men's and women's court testimony would be considered equal, although it is unclear to what extent this will apply to personal-status cases. A draft labor law in the UAE, if passed, would specifically prohibit discrimination between people with equal qualifications and ban termination of employment on the basis of marital status, pregnancy, or maternity.

Throughout the region, however, the prevailing patriarchal attitudes, prejudice, and traditional leanings of male judges, lawyers, and court officials—as well as the lack of an independent judiciary that is capable of upholding basic rights despite political or societal pressure—threaten to undermine these new legal protections. Unless effective complaint mechanisms are in place and the appropriate court personnel are trained to apply justice in a gender-blind manner, the new laws will not achieve the desired effect. Moreover, unless the judicial system of each country becomes more independent, rigorous, and professional, women of high social standing will continue to have better access to justice than poor women and domestic workers.

"We [in the West] need to appreciate that all kinds of women in the Muslim world might . . . see the charges of the oppression of Muslim women as absurd."

The West Misrepresents the Oppression of Middle Eastern Women

Lila Abu-Lughod

In the following viewpoint, an anthropology professor refutes West-ern images that stereotype Middle Eastern women as oppressed and powerless. She believes the prevalent images do not adequately reflect the diversity of women in the region. For example, she claims that the traditional burqa, or outer garment worn by women that covers the body has been turned into a symbol of subjugation by Western observers. She argues that the West must recognize that women in the Middle East—like women in all countries—are fight-ing for equality in a manner that reflects their respect for culture and community. Lila Abu-Lughod is a professor of anthropology and women's and gender studies at Columbia University. She has focused much of her studies on the Arab world.

Lila Abu-Lughod, "The Muslim Woman: The Power of Images and the Danger of Pity," *Lettre Internationale*, vol. 12, 2006. First published in Danish in *Lettre Internationale* (DK) and in English in *Eurozine* (www.eurozine.com). Copyright © 2006 by Lila Abu-Lughod. All rights reserved. Reproduced by permission.

As you read, consider the following questions:

1. Why does anthropologist Hanna Papanek view the burqa as "liberating," according to this viewpoint?

2. What does the Western feminists' mission to "save" Middle Eastern women not-so-subtly reinforce, in Abu-Lughod's opinion?

3. What two points does Abu-Lughod mention that were put forth by a new global studies textbook on Islam rebutting Western charges that Islam is sexist?

What images do we, in the United States or Europe, have of Muslim women, or women from the region known as the Middle East? Our lives are saturated with images, images that are strangely confined to a very limited set of tropes or themes. The oppressed Muslim woman. The veiled Muslim woman. The Muslim woman who does not have the same freedoms we have. The woman ruled by her religion. The woman ruled by her men.

These images have a long history in the West but they have become especially visible and persistent since 9/11. Many women in the US mobilized around the cause of the Afghani women oppressed by the fundamentalist Taliban [religious government regime]—women who were represented in the media as covered from head to toe in their *burqas* [a robe-like garment used to cover the whole body], unable to go to school or wear nail polish. An administration—George W. Bush's—then used the oppression of these Muslim women as part of the moral justification for the military invasion of Afghanistan. These images of veiled and oppressed women have been used to drum up support for intervention. Besides the untold horrors, dislocations, and violence these US interventions have brought to the lives of Muslim women in Afghanistan and Iraq, I would argue that the use of these images has also been bad for us, in the countries of the West where they circulate, because of the deadening effect they have on our capacity to appreciate the complexity and diversity of Muslim women's lives—as human beings.

Misleading Images of Middle Eastern Women

As the late [cultural critic] Edward Said pointed out in his famous book, *Orientalism*, a transformative and critical study of the relationship between the Western study of the Middle East and the Muslim world and the larger projects of dominating or colonizing these regions, one of the most distinctive qualities of representations—literary and scholarly—of the Muslim "East" has been their citationary nature. What he meant by this is that later works gain authority by citing earlier ones, referring to each other in an endless chain that has no need for the actualities of the Muslim East. We can see this even today in visual representations of the Muslim woman. I have been collecting such images for years, ones that reveal clearly the citationary quality of images of "the Muslim woman". The most iconic are those I think of as studies in black and white. One finds, for example, impenetrable Algerian women shrouded in ghostly white in the French colonial postcards from the 1930s that [Algerian writer and critic] Malek Alloula analyzes in his book, *The Colonial Harem*. This kind of photography, Alloula argues, was dedicated to making Algerian women accessible, if only symbolically, to French soldiers, tourists, and the people back home. And then one finds in the late 1990s covers of American media, even highbrow, such as the *New York Times Magazine* or the *Chronicle of Higher Education*, that similarly depict women whose faces are hidden and bodies covered in white or pale Islamic modest dress. These are women from Jordan or Egypt whose lives and situations are radically unlike those of women in colonial Algeria, and unlike many other women in their own countries. One also finds in Alloula's book of postcards images of women dressed dramatically in black, with only eyes showing. Again, almost identical images appear on the covers of the *New York Times Magazine* and even *KLM Magazine*

[Dutch airlines magazine] from 1990 to the present, despite the fact that the articles they are linked to are on different countries: Saudi Arabia, Jordan, and Yemen. There is an amazing uniformity.

Why should we find this disturbing? I certainly feel uncomfortable with my collection of media images because my twenty-five years of experience doing research in the Middle East, especially Egypt, has taught me that images like these do not reflect the variety of styles of women's dress in those countries and do nothing to convey the meaning of these differences. My own family albums include photos of my Palestinian grandmother and aunt in one of these countries—Jordan—my aunt wearing a blouse and slacks, her long straight hair uncovered; even my grandmother has just a simple white scarf draped loosely over her hair. They also include an old photo of my grandmother and aunt and two of my uncles taken sometime in the 1950s, the men in suits and the women in neat dresses, their hair nicely coiffed. Even if one turns to recent news items from these countries, take Jordan for example, again, one finds small photos that include the national women's basketball team in shorts or the Queen dining with a group of other cosmopolitan women, European and Jordanian, and you can't tell the difference. Why are these not on the cover of the *New York Times Magazine*, representing Jordan, instead of the shrouded woman?

Moreover, it is odd that in many of the images from the media, the veiled women stand in for the countries the articles are about. None of these articles in the *New York Times Magazine*, for example, was about Muslim women, or even Jordanian or Egyptian women. It would be as if magazines and newspapers in Syria or Malaysia were to put bikini clad women or Madonna on every cover of a magazine that featured an article about the United States or a European country.

Ignoring the Diversity of Women in the Region

There are several problems with these uniform and ubiquitous images of veiled women. First, they make it hard to think about the Muslim world without thinking about women, creating a seemingly huge divide between "us" and "them" based on the treatment or positions of women. This prevents us from thinking about the connections between our various parts of the world, helping setting up a civilizational divide. Second, they make it hard to appreciate the variety of women's lives across the Muslim or Middle Eastern worlds—differences of time and place and differences of class and region. Third, they even make it hard for us to appreciate that veiling itself is a complex practice.

Let me take a little time over this third point. It is common knowledge that the ultimate sign of the oppression of Afghani women under the Taliban-and-the-terrorists is that they were forced to wear the *burqa*. Liberals sometimes confess their surprise that even though Afghanistan has been liberated from the Taliban, women do not seem to be throwing off their *burqas*. Someone like me, who has worked in Muslim regions, asks why this is so surprising. Did we expect that once "free" from the Taliban they would go "back" to belly shirts and blue jeans, or dust off their Chanel suits?

We need to recall some basics of veiling. First, the Taliban did not invent the *burqa* in Afghanistan. It was the local form of covering that Pashtun women in one region wore when they went out. The Pashtun are one of several ethnic groups in Afghanistan and the *burqa* was one of many forms of covering in the subcontinent and Southwest Asia that has developed as a convention for symbolizing women's modesty or respectability. The *burqa*, like some other forms of "cover" has, in many settings, marked the symbolic separation of men's and women's spheres, as part of the general association of women with family and home, not with public space where strangers mingled.

A Cultural Marker of Respectability

Twenty-some years ago, the anthropologist Hanna Papanek, who worked in Pakistan, described the *burqa* as "portable seclusion". She noted that many saw it as a liberating invention since it enabled women to move out of segregated living spaces while still observing the basic moral requirements of separating and protecting women from unrelated men. Ever since I came across her phrase "portable seclusion", I have thought of these enveloping robes as "mobile homes". Everywhere, such veiling signifies belonging to a particular community and participating in a moral way of life in which families are paramount in the organization of communities and the home is associated with the sanctity of women.

The obvious question that follows is: if this is the case, why would women suddenly become immodest? Why would they suddenly throw off the markers of their respectability, markers, whether *burqas* or other forms of cover, that were supposed to assure their protection in the public sphere from the harassment of strange men by symbolically signalling that they were still in the inviolable space of their homes, even though moving in the public realm? Especially when these are forms of dress that had become so conventional that most women gave little thought to their meaning?

To draw some analogies, none perfect: why are we surprised when Afghan women don't throw off their *burqas* when we know perfectly well that it wouldn't be appropriate to wear shorts to the opera? Religious belief and community standards of propriety require the covering of the hair in some traditions—Muslim, Jewish, and Catholic until recently. People wear the appropriate form of dress for their social communities and are guided by socially shared standards, religious beliefs, and moral ideals, unless they deliberately transgress to make a point or are unable to afford proper cover. If we think that American women, even the nonreligious, live in a world of choice regarding clothing, all we need to do is remind ourselves of the expression, "the tyranny of fashion".

What had happened in Afghanistan under the Taliban is that one regional style of covering or veiling, associated with a certain respectable but not elite class, was imposed on everyone as "religiously" appropriate, even though previously there had been many different styles, popular or traditional with different groups and classes—different ways to mark women's propriety, or, in more recent times, religious piety. Although I am not an expert on Afghanistan, I imagine that the majority of women left in Afghanistan by the time the Taliban took control were the rural or less educated, from non-elite families, since they were the only ones who couldn't emigrate to escape the hardship and violence that has marked Afghanistan's recent history. If liberated from the enforced wearing of *burqas*, most of these women would choose some other form of modest head covering, like all those living nearby who were not under the Taliban—their rural Hindu counterparts in the North of India (who cover their heads and veil their faces from relatives by marriage) or their Muslim sisters in Pakistan. Some there wear gauzy scarves, some the newer forms of Islamic modest dress.

I want to make a crucial point about veiling here. Not only are there many forms of covering which themselves have different meanings in the communities in which they are used, but veiling itself must not be confused with, or made to stand for, lack of agency. As I have argued in *Veiled Sentiments*, my ethnography of a Bedouin community in Egypt in the late 1970s and 1980s, pulling the black headcloth over the face in front of older respected men is considered a voluntary act by women who are deeply committed to being moral and have a sense of honour tied to family. One of the ways they show their self-respect and social standing is by covering their faces in certain contexts. And they decide for whom they feel it is appropriate to veil. They don't veil for younger men; they don't veil for foreign men. They don't even veil for Egyptian non-Bedouin men because they don't respect them and don't, in the latter two cases, consider these men as part of their moral community. . . .

The Danger of Speaking on Behalf of Middle Eastern Women

I have argued that the power of these images of veiled women is that they dull our understanding and restrict our appreciation of complexity. The second half of the [original] subtitle of this essay is "the danger of pity". What does pity have to do with Muslim or Middle Eastern women? It seems obvious to me that one of the most dangerous functions of these images of Middle Eastern or Muslim women is to enable many of us to imagine that these women need rescuing by us or by our governments.

I first began to think about pity when I ran across a book many years ago at the Princeton Theological Seminary; it was the proceedings of a Presbyterian women's missionary conference held in Cairo, Egypt, in 1906. It was a collection of many chapters on the sad plight of the Mohammedan woman (as she was known then) in countries from Egypt to Indonesia, detailing the lack of love in her marriage, her ignorance, her subjection to polygamy, her seclusion, and the symbolic evidence of her low status in her veiling. In the introduction to this book, graphically called *Our Moslem Sisters: A Cry of Need from Lands of Darkness Interpreted by Those Who Heard It*, Annie Van Sommer, speaking on behalf of her fellow women missionaries (and of course appealing for financial support for the good works of these women missionaries), explains: "This book with its sad, reiterated story of wrong and oppression is an indictment and an appeal [. . .] It is an appeal to Christian womanhood to right these wrongs and enlighten this darkness by sacrifice and service." She goes on to say: "It seems to some of us that it needs the widespread love and pity of the women of our day in Christian lands to seek and save the suffering sinful needy women of Islam. You cannot know how great the need unless you are told; you will never go and find them until you hear their cry." Western Christian women at the turn of the century thus saw themselves as voicing what Muslim women cannot, or amplifying the stifled voices of these "others" in the service of Christian salvation. This, of course, is in Victorian times when women didn't have the vote, were rarely in the public sphere, were supposed to have been angels in the house. The missionary women were unusually independent and adventurous, though often they went as wives.

One can worry about the echoes of this rhetoric in contemporary liberal feminist concerns about women around the world. One need only think of the American organization the Feminist Majority, with their campaign for the women in Afghanistan, or the wider discourse about women's human rights. Like the missionaries, these liberal feminists feel the need to speak for and on behalf of Afghan or other Muslim women in a language of women's rights or human rights. They see themselves as an enlightened group with the vision and freedom to help suffering women elsewhere to receive their rights, to rescue them from their men or from their oppressive religious traditions.

If one constructs some women as being in need of pity or saving, one implies that one not only wants to save them from something but wants to save them for something—a different kind of world and set of arrangements. What violences might be entailed in this transformation? And what presumptions are being made about the superiority of what you are saving them for? Projects to save other women, of whatever kind, depend on and reinforce Westerners' sense of superiority. They also smack of a form of patronizing arrogance that, as an anthropologist who is sensitive to other ways of living, makes me feel uncomfortable. I've spent lots of time with different groups of Muslim women and know something about how they see themselves, how they respect themselves, and how I admire and love them as complex and resourceful women.

My point is that perhaps we ought to be more aware of different paths in this world. Maybe we should consider being respectful of other routes towards social change. Is it impossible to ask whether there can be a liberation that is Islamic? This idea is being explored by many women, like those in Iran, who call themselves Islamic feminists. And beyond this, is liberation or freedom even a goal for which all women or people strive? Are emancipation, equality, and rights part of a universal language? Might other desires be more meaningful for different groups of people? Such as living in close families? Such as living in a godly way? Such as living without war or violence?

Western Hypocrisy

There are other perspectives, some of which question Western superiority. For example, addressing himself to the United States, one notorious Islamist [Osama bin Laden] accuses: "You are a nation that exploits women like consumer products or advertising tools, calling upon customers to purchase them. You use women to serve passengers, visitors, and strangers to increase your profit margins. You then rant that you support the liberation of women [. . .] You are a nation that practices the trade of sex in all its forms, directly and indirectly. Giant corporations and establishments are established on this, under the name of art, entertainment, tourism, and freedom, and other deceptive names that you attribute to it."

More moderate Muslim apologists also defend Islam against accusations by Westerners of sexism. In a new global studies textbook on Islam, the section called "Islam is sexist" contains a twenty-eight-point rebuttal of this charge. This rebuttal gives explanations of Quranic verses, describes the Prophet Muhammad's position on various aspects of women's status, provides observations about how late women were given the vote in some European countries (Switzerland in 1971, for example), and notes how many Muslim women have governed countries (five prime ministers or presidents in Pakistan, Bangladesh, Turkey, and Indonesia) compared to none, for example, in the United States.

Is what these apologists describe by way of sexual exploitation or lack of public power a reason to pity American or European women? We would find this either absurd or annoying. We have a million answers to their charges. Even if we are critical of the treatment of women in our own societies in Europe or the United States, whether we talk about the glass ceiling that keeps women professionals from rising to the top, the system that keeps so many women-headed households below the poverty line, the high incidence of rape and sexual harassment, or even the exploitation of women in advertising, we do not see this as reflective of the oppressiveness of our culture or a reason to condemn Christianity—the dominant religious tradition. We know such things have complicated causes and we know that some of us, at least, are working to change things.

Similarly, we need to appreciate that all kinds of women in the Muslim world might also see the charges of the oppression of Muslim women as absurd, or annoying. This would include ordinary women like those I've lived with in rural areas and the feminists and other reformers who have, since the late nineteenth century, seen problems in their own societies regarding the position of women. We have to be careful not to fall into polarizations that place feminism only on the side of the West. . . .

Recognizing Rights from a Middle Eastern Woman's Perspective

But I want to make another point: not only are Muslim women engaged in projects for women's rights in terms that we recognize, but many women in other parts of the world don't necessarily see their lives as deficient in terms of rights. I'm not talking about self-delusion and false consciousness—that the women don't see their own oppression. I'm arguing that we need to recognize and perhaps even be able to appreciate the different terms in which people live their lives. In my book *Writing Women's Worlds*, which I think of as an experimental "feminist" ethnography of the Awlad 'Ali Bedouin women in Egypt I lived with in the early 1980s, I tried to tell women's stories in the terms they used. I also tried to capture the criteria they used for judging others and putting forward claims.

Stories of marriage offer the best evidence both of the inaptness of the opposition between choice and constraint that dominates our understanding of the differences between Western and Muslim women and of the importance of recognizing different constructions of "rights". Girls I knew in this Bedouin community resisted particular marriages that were arranged for them but never the basic principle that families should arrange marriages. They might sing songs about the kind of young men they wanted to marry—those who were not cousins, those who were educated, those riding in certain kinds of cars and trucks—but they assumed that it was up to their families to choose such matches for them. They even made trouble when they didn't want a particular husband, often subverting or undermining a marriage arranged for them. But even the love poems that I wrote my first book about, *Veiled Sentiments*, poems that registered their longings and frustrations, were a mode of expression fully within a system, not a rebellion against a system that arranged marriage, that required women to preserve their honour by not showing any interest in men, or that expected men and women not to show affection in public, even when married. Many girls and mothers told me about the dangers of love matches; all valued the protections and support afforded by their families in arranged marriages. More interesting, women in marriages often asserted "rights"—based on some sense of Islamic and customary law but mostly derived from a keen sense of justice they had internalized through watching community practices but also from ingrained expectations about their self-worth and their responsibilities. This happened in cases when husbands treated them badly.

An even better example of the problem of assuming we know what rights women want is the case of polygyny in this community. A whole chapter of my book *Writing Women's Worlds* attends to the shifting relationships, solidarities, angers, and sorrows in one polygamous marriage that I knew intimately. It wasn't the fact of a husband marrying more than one wife that was ever the issue for these particular co-wives. This practice was supported in Islamic law and recognized as something that happened for various reasons, including a desire for children or providing for unsupported women. Instead, it was the particular personalities, histories, behaviours, and feelings for each other that mattered to the women. The reproach and claim of one co-wife, after telling me a long story about an infuriating situation that she found herself in just after her husband married his third wife, was different from what I would have imagined or expected. I had asked her, sympathetically, at the end of this story, if she'd been jealous. She answered right away: "No I wasn't jealous. I was just angry that we were being treated unfairly. Aren't we all the same?" This is hardly a liberal argument for women's human rights or an argument about the oppressiveness of polygyny. It is an argument that co-wives have the right, according to the Qur'an and Bedouin ideals, to be treated with absolute equality. . . .

Differences Should Be Respected

Choices for all of us are fashioned by discourses, social locations, geopolitical configurations, and unequal power into historically and locally specific ranges. Those for whom religious values are important certainly don't see them as constraining—they see them as ideals for which to strive.

We may want justice for women but can we accept that there might be different ideas about justice and that different women might want, or choose, different futures from what we envision as best? And that the choices they see before them are in fact a product of some situations we have helped foist on them? My conclusion is that if we do care about the situations of women different from white middle class Western women, we would do well to leave behind veils and vocations of saving others and instead train our sights on ways to make the world a more just place.

Periodical and Internet Sources Bibliography

The following articles have been chosen to supplement the diverse views presented in this chapter.

Penny Andrews	"Sixty Years On: The International Human Rights Movement Today," *Maryland Journal of International Law*, January 2009.
John Dietrich and Caitlyn Witkowski	"Obama's Human Rights Policy: Déjà vu with a Twist," *Human Rights Review*, March 2012.
Muhammad Tariq Ghauri	"Scope of Human Rights in Islam: An Analytical Study of Islamic Concept of Human Rights," *Dialogue*, October–December 2010.
Li Guowen	"China's Human Rights Cause Based on Traditional Chinese Culture," *China Today*, November 2011.
Margaret E. McGuinness	"Peace v. Justice: The Universal Declaration of Human Rights and the Modern Origins of the Debate," *Diplomatic History*, November 2011.
Irene Oh	"Islamic Voices and the Definition of Human Rights," *Journal of Church and State*, September 2011.
A. Byaruhanga Rukooko	"Poverty and Human Rights in Africa: Historical Dynamics and the Case for Economic Social and Cultural Rights," *International Journal of Human Rights*, February 2010.
Megan Shank and Jeffrey Wasserstrom	"Anxious Times in a Rising China: Lurching toward a New Social Compact," *Dissent*, Winter 2012.
Caroline Walsh	"Taking Account of Violations: Rethinking Equality and Human Rights," *Journal of Human Rights*, April–June 2012.

OPPOSING
VIEWPOINTS®
SERIES

CHAPTER 2

How Should the US Government Address Human Rights Issues?

Chapter Preface

On May 24, 2012, the US State Department released its annual report on human rights worldwide. The document criticized several countries for poor performance in safeguarding the rights of their citizens or actively abridging some of those rights. The review of China's human rights record, however, became a subject of political contention. The report indicted China for silencing civil rights activists. The State Department also maintained, "Individuals and groups seen as politically sensitive by the authorities continued to face tight restrictions on their freedom to assemble, practice religion, and travel." The day after the report was released, China struck back, releasing its own report on the "woeful" state of human rights in the United States. The Chinese report accused US authorities of cracking down on the Occupy Wall Street protestors rallying against economic and social inequality. It also singled out the USA Patriot Act legislation, signed by George W. Bush and extended by Barack Obama, which expanded the government's authority to monitor and investigate suspicious Internet use. Citing the continued presence of racism and discrimination, the report insisted, "The United States' tarnished human rights record has left it in no state—whether on a moral, political or legal basis—to act as the world's 'human rights justice.'"

Although US authorities typically ignore such chiding, domestic critics have leveled similar accusations. Amnesty International, for instance, has written news releases on the plight of migrant workers in the United States and has condemned the government's detention (and in some case, torture) of alleged terrorists and enemy combatants from the wars in Afghanistan and Iraq. How the United States responds to such charges is significant in clarifying where the nation stands on these issues and what moral leadership it can pledge to the international community. In the 2010–2011 Universal Periodic Review conducted by the US State Department in conjunction with the UN Human Rights Council, the drafters assert that the United States has always been a grand experiment in democracy with a respect for human rights codified in the US Constitution. The review states, "Throughout our history, our citizens have used the freedoms provided in the Constitution as a foundation upon which to advocate for changes that would create a more just society. . . . Human rights—including the freedoms of speech, association, and religion—have empowered our people to be the engine of our progress."

The Universal Periodic Review speaks of the progress the nation has made toward bringing equality to all citizens and ending discrimination. According to the document, the nation has shown its commitment to equal participation and representation, for example, by appointing ethnic and sexual minorities to key government positions. "And while individual stories do not prove the absence of enduring challenges," the drafters attest, "they demonstrate the presence of possibilities." The review even confronts issues such as torture and electronic surveillance of citizens, insisting that the former is not tolerated and that the latter has passed strict congressional scrutiny. The review concludes with the assurance that "we welcome observations and recommendations that can help us on that road to a more perfect union."

The authors in the following chapter examine the US government's commitment to protecting human rights. They debate how effectively the nation has turned words into deeds in regards to the equal treatment of its citizens, the preservation of privacy, and how well the nation's human rights ideals have translated to its role in ensuring global justice.

"[Joining the International Criminal Court] . . . would reinforce Obama administration statements about participating fully in multilateral institutions."

The United States Should Join the International Criminal Court

Butch Bracknell

In the following viewpoint, a US marine contends that the United States is losing global credibility by resisting joining the International Criminal Court (ICC), a judicial body established in 2002 to try cases of war crimes and other abuses against humanity. The author believes the United States cannot continue to preach multilateralism and global cooperation if it refuses to become party to the seat of global law. Butch Bracknell is a US marine lieutenant and a senior fellow at the Atlantic Council, a US-European partnership advocacy organization that addresses issues of global security, energy concerns, and other international matters.

As you read, consider the following questions:

1. What is the name of the statute that inaugurated the International Criminal Court?
2. Why did the Bill Clinton and George W. Bush administrations refuse to ratify the ICC treaty, according to Bracknell?
3. Why does Bracknell believe that the United States has little to fear from potential ICC indictments against US citizens?

I recently returned from a week in Iraq, where I trained an elite security force unit on human rights and the law of combat operations. Discussions regarding the responsibility of commanders for the acts of their forces migrated to the issue of the United Nations' International Criminal Court [ICC]. One Iraqi officer asked me, "If the United States believes in accountability over impunity, why are you not a party to the International Criminal Court?" I did not have a satisfactory answer.

The answer for public consumption is that U.S. accession to the Rome Statute, which established the International Criminal Court, is not an imminent issue because U.S. processes for achieving accountability function well: The military and civilian courts are open, the government already is bringing cases to court where the evidence warrants, and convictions are occurring on a sufficiently regular basis. The subtext is that the [Barack] Obama administration has to prioritize where to spend political capital and carefully select its fights. Nonetheless, as a nation, we need to revive the debate over joining the ICC.

Proving U.S. Commitment to Multilateralism

The National Security Strategy and other key U.S. foreign affairs and security policy documents stress the merits of multilateralism, international partnership and working through institutions to achieve desirable foreign policy outcomes. American failure to join the ICC is a holdover from unilateralist ideologues in the George W. Bush administration. This failure is inconsistent with current U.S. national policy, which touts the ICC as a viable and appropriate forum for filing charges against Sudan's Omar Hassan Ahmed Bashir and his Darfur co-conspirators; Kenyan Deputy Prime Minister Uhuru Kenyatta; Lord's Resistance Army chairman Joseph Kony in Uganda; Libyan regime leaders, including Moammar Kadafi, his son Saif Islam and his intelligence chief; and other corrupt strongmen who misuse governmental power for personal and political advantage.[1]

Signing and ratifying the statute before the 2012 election would permit the Obama administration to act on its stated intentions to use multilateralism and international institutions as proxies for costly and treacherous U.S. unilateralism. Acceding to the Rome Statute would demonstrate leadership to our allies and set a strategic tone of multilateralism at low political cost and risk.

Opponents Placed U.S. Fears Before U.S. Interests

Though the U.S. signed the treaty in 2000 to preserve the ability to shape the statute's evolution, both the [Bill] Clinton and Bush administrations publicly opposed ratifying the ICC on the grounds that the Rome Statute compromises national sovereignty. Its critics contend the court could subject U.S. troops and officials to the jurisdiction of a politically motivated prosecutor, who would use the court's jurisdiction over an American service member or public official to make a political point against the United States.

The Bush administration and, later, Congress conditioned certain military cooperation and aid on the execution of agreements that bound the partner states not to surrender U.S. personnel to the jurisdiction of the ICC. Strong-arming allies desperate

How US Support Would Benefit the ICC Mission

US support for the long-term success of the International Criminal Court is critical. Support the US can bring to the process will come in many forms. First and foremost is the funding of the court. America is the most prosperous nation in the world and the US contributes roughly twenty five percent of the UN's current operational budget. Contributing an equivalent percentage amount to the court will go a long way to its long-term success of the court. As it stands now, the court is funded from three sources: contributions from States' parties, voluntary contributions, and from the UN, as approved by the General Assembly but not including US UN dues. A second critical piece that the US can provide to the Court is intelligence. American intelligence is crucial. . . . The third aspect that the US can bring to ensure success to the court is judicial and prosecutorial personnel. No other nation in the world has the quality and number of lawyers and judges that the US has, nor does any state have the number and quality of personnel that could serve as prosecutors and investigators in the service of the court.

Jeffrey Wiley, "Why Is the US Afraid of the International Criminal Court?," Strategy Research Project of the US Army War College, March 15, 2008.

for U.S. cooperation placed narrow and shallow U.S. interests over real partnership, which is more valuable to long-term American interests. That stance against the court's jurisdiction was really a proxy statement for U.S. unilateralism—strategic messaging that the U.S. would not yield even a small amount of U.S. sovereignty to multilateral institutions or processes, even where the tradeoff could be substantially positive.

The United States Has Little to Fear from ICC Jurisdiction

The ICC poses extraordinarily low risk to U.S. sovereignty, service members and public officials abroad. Under the Rome Statute's "complementarity" principle, before the court asserts jurisdiction over a citizen, the ICC prosecutor must determine and substantiate that the citizen's country is operating with impunity or that its judicial processes are broken or powerless. To avoid ICC jurisdiction over American service members and public officials, the United States would not have to charge, indict and bring cases to court. All that is required is for the U.S. to undertake a good-faith investigative effort of offenses under the statute and domestic law, and meaningfully assert national jurisdiction over alleged offenses.

The Rome Statute merely confirms our national social and legal instincts: to address unlawful activity appropriately and within an evenhanded, legitimate legal framework. As long as U.S. processes continue to operate and set the world standard for impartial investigations and just exercise of prosecutorial discretion, the U.S. has little to fear from the ICC.

With or without the United States, the ICC will continue to hold accountable rogue world leaders and public officials whose conduct violates the legal standards established by the Rome Statute. For certain world leaders accustomed to acting with impunity, it is the court of last resort. Acceding to and ratifying the Rome Statute would enable the U.S. to participate in future deliberations on the evolution of the statute. It also would reinforce Obama administration statements about participating fully in multilateral institutions and lend credence to administration positions on the utility of the ICC in thwarting impunity by treacherous leaders, such as Kenyan ethnic warlords and the Libyan inner circle.

Absent accession to the Rome Statute, the message America sends to the world is unprincipled: The U.S. is committed to the concept of multilateralism—except when it is not.

Notes

1. Bashir is accused of aiding the ethnic cleansing of non-Afro-Arabs in the Darfur region of Sudan. Kenyatta is accused of instigating violence after the Kenyan election of 2007. Kony, a guerilla leader, was indicted by the ICC for war crimes. The Kadafi regime is accused of war crimes occurring during the 2011 overthrow of that government.

> *"While the International Criminal Court represents an admirable desire to hold war criminals accountable for their terrible crimes, the court is flawed notionally and operationally."*

The United States Should Not Join the International Criminal Court

Brett D. Schaefer and Steven Groves

In the following viewpoint, two political analysts caution government officials who may be considering committing the United States to membership in the International Criminal Court (ICC). The authors insist that the ICC seems to serve the worthy goal of prosecuting war crimes, but they warn that its methods and broad powers do not currently serve US interests. Until the ICC corrects some of its shortcomings, the authors contend, the United States should continue to refrain from joining this body. Brett D. Schaefer is a fellow in international regulatory affairs at the Heritage Foundation, a conservative public policy think-tank. Steven Groves is also a member of the Heritage Foundation, serving as a fellow in its Kathryn and Shelby Cullom Davis Institute for International Studies.

As you read, consider the following questions:

1. Why do Schaefer and Groves maintain that the ICC has not been a deterrent to individuals or nations pursuing actions that would be deemed war crimes?

2. Why do the authors believe granting the ICC authority to punish individuals for crimes of "aggression" is questionable and unwise?

3. According to Schaefer and Groves, why was it potentially counterproductive for the ICC to issue a warrant for the arrest of Sudanese President Omar Bashir?

The idea of establishing an international court to prosecute serious international crimes—war crimes, crimes against humanity, and genocide—has long held a special place in the hearts of human rights activists and those hoping to hold perpetrators of terrible crimes to account. In 1998, that idea became reality when the Rome Statute of the International Criminal Court was adopted at a diplomatic conference convened by the U.N. General Assembly. The International Criminal Court (ICC) was formally established in 2002 after 60 countries ratified the statute. The ICC was created to prosecute war crimes, crimes against humanity, genocide, and the as yet undefined crime of aggression. Regrettably, although the court's supporters have a noble purpose, there are a number of reasons to be cautious and concerned about how ratification of the Rome Statute would affect U.S. sovereignty and how ICC action could affect politically precarious situations around the world.

Among other concerns, past U.S. Administrations concluded that the Rome Statute created a seriously flawed institution that lacks prudent safeguards against political manipulation, possesses sweeping authority without accountability to the U.N. Security Council, and violates national sovereignty by claiming jurisdiction over the nationals and military personnel of non-party states in some circumstances. These concerns led

President Bill Clinton to urge President George W. Bush not to submit the treaty to the Senate for advice and consent necessary for ratification. After extensive efforts to change the statute to address key U.S. concerns failed, President Bush felt it necessary to "un-sign" the Rome Statute by formally notifying the U.N. Secretary-General that the U.S. did not intend to ratify the treaty and was no longer bound under international law to avoid actions that would run counter to the intent and purpose of the treaty. Subsequently, the U.S. took a number of steps to protect its military personnel, officials, and nationals from ICC claims of jurisdiction. . . .

The ICC Has a Broad Jurisdiction

The International Criminal Court has a clear legal lineage extending back to the Nuremburg and Tokyo trials and ad hoc tribunals, such as the ICTY [the International Criminal Tribunal for the former Yugoslavia] and the ICTR [the International Criminal Tribunal for Rwanda], which were established by the U.N. Security Council in 1993 and 1994, respectively. However, the ICC is much broader and more independent than these limited precedents. Its authority is not limited to disputes between governments as is the case with the International Court of Justice (ICJ) or to a particular jurisdiction as is the case with national judiciaries. Nor is its authority limited to particular crimes committed in a certain place or period of time as was the case with the post-World War II trials and the Yugoslavian and Rwandan tribunals.

Instead, the ICC claims jurisdiction over individuals committing genocide, crimes against humanity, war crimes, and the undefined crime of aggression. This jurisdiction extends from the entry into force of the Rome Statute in July 2002 and applies to all citizens of states that have ratified the Rome Statute. However, it also extends to individuals from countries that are not party to the Rome Statute if the alleged crimes occur on the territory of an ICC party state, the non-party government invites

ICC jurisdiction, or the U.N. Security Council refers the case to the ICC.

International lawyers Lee Casey and David Rivkin point out that the ICC is a radical departure from previous international courts: The ICC represents a fundamental break with the past. It has jurisdiction over individuals, including elected or appointed government officials, and its judgments may be directly enforced against them, regardless of their own national constitutions or court systems. Unlike the ICJ, the ICC has the very real potential to shape the policies of its member states in the substantive areas where it operates. These include the core issues of when states can lawfully resort to armed force, how that force may be applied, and whether particular actions constitute the very serious international offenses of war crimes, crimes against humanity, or genocide.

Moreover, although it is generally considered to be within the U.N. family, the ICC is not explicitly a U.N. body. It is an independent treaty body overseen by the states that have ratified the Rome Statute. . . .

The ICC Lacks Checks and Balances

The court's structure establishes few, if any, practical external checks on the ICC's authority. Among the judges' responsibilities are determining whether the prosecutor may proceed with a case and whether a member state has been "unwilling or unable genuinely to carry out the investigation or prosecution," which would trigger the ICC's jurisdiction under the principle of "complementarity," which is designed to limit the court's power and avoid political abuse of its authority. Thus, the various arms of the ICC are themselves the only real check on its authority. This absence of external checks raises serious concerns [as Casey and Rivkin state]:

> The ability both to interpret the law and effectively to force member states to adopt its view gives the ICC unprecedented

power. For the first time, a permanent international institution is entitled to determine the legal obligations of states and their individual citizens and to criminally punish those individual citizens—even if its understanding of the law radically differs from the relevant state's position. Moreover, the ICC's judges are not otherwise subject to the supervision or control of the states' parties, except in matters of personal corruption. Thus, when the ICC determines what international law requires in any of its areas of competence, this is arguably the final word. . . .

The Court Has Not Been a Deterrent to War Crimes

As an institution, the ICC has performed little, if any, better than the ad hoc tribunals that it was created to replace. Like the Rwandan and Yugoslavian tribunals, the ICC is slow to act. The ICC prosecutor took six months to open an investigation in Uganda, two months with the DRC [Democratic Republic of Congo], over a year with Darfur [Sudan], and nearly two years with the Central African Republic. It has yet to conclude a full trial cycle more than seven years after being created. Moreover, like the ad hoc tribunals, the ICC can investigate and prosecute crimes only after the fact. The alleged deterrent effect of a standing international criminal court has not ended atrocities in the DRC, Uganda, the Central African Republic, or Darfur, where cases are ongoing. Nor has it deterred atrocities by Burma against its own people, crimes committed during Russia's 2008 invasion of Georgia (an ICC party), ICC party Venezuela's support of leftist guerillas in Colombia, or any of a number of other situations around the world where war crimes or crimes against humanity may be occurring.

Another problem is that the ICC lacks a mechanism to enforce its rulings and is, therefore, entirely dependent on governments to arrest and transfer perpetrators to the court. However, such arrests can have significant diplomatic consequences, which can greatly inhibit the efficacy of the court in pursuing its warrants and prosecuting outstanding cases. The most prominent example is Sudanese President [Omar] Bashir's willingness to travel to other countries on official visits—thus far only to non-ICC states—despite the ICC arrest warrant [for his alleged encouragement of ethnic cleansing in Darfur]. This flaw was also present with the ICTY and the ICTR, although they could at least rely on a Security Council resolution mandating international cooperation in enforcing their arrest warrants. . . .

U.S. Cooperation with the ICC

Many of the flaws in the Rome Statute identified by the Clinton and Bush Administrations remain unaddressed. Although the U.S. has reserved the option of cooperating with the ICC in certain circumstances, it has repeatedly stated that fundamental changes to the Rome Statute are needed before the U.S. could ratify the treaty. The U.S. has taken legislative and diplomatic steps to protect U.S. citizens, officials, and military personnel from the ICC's jurisdiction, which the U.S. considers illegitimate. These steps in no way violate international law. On the contrary, they bolster international law by complying with international legal norms and rules as they have been traditionally understood.

Moreover, these actions do not preclude the U.S. from supporting an ICC investigation when it is deemed important to U.S. interests. The most pertinent example is the Bush Administration's decision not to block U.N. Security Council Resolution 1593, which referred the situation in Darfur to the ICC. The U.S. abstention acknowledged that the existence of the court and many states' support for the ICC would not be changed by the U.S. vetoing every Security Council resolution that references the ICC. It demonstrated a pragmatic approach of weighing the costs and benefits of U.S. policy toward the ICC against other interests and echoed President Bush's use of his waiver authority under ASPA [American Service-Members' Protection Act of 2002] and the

Nethercutt Amendment [2005 fiscal legislation that prohibited aid to ICC members unless they agreed never to surrender U.S. citizens to the court] when those restrictions undermined other U.S. interests. However, it did not change the U.S. effort to protect its nationals from the ICC's illegitimate jurisdictional claims. Indeed, the U.S. abstention was secured only after language protecting U.S. persons from the ICC was included in the resolution:

> [N]ationals, current or former officials or personnel from a contributing State outside Sudan which is not a party to the Rome Statute of the International Criminal Court shall be subject to the exclusive jurisdiction of that contributing State for all alleged acts or omissions arising out of or related to operations in Sudan established or authorized by the Council or the African Union, unless such exclusive jurisdiction has been expressly waived by that contributing State. . . .

Until the U.S. formally joins the ICC, legislative and policy measures to protect U.S. military personnel, officials, and nationals from the ICC are entirely prudent and warranted. Indeed, recent instances of national courts and prosecutors asserting extraterritorial jurisdiction, such as those by judicial authorities in Spain and the Netherlands, underscore the need for the U.S. to protect itself and its citizens and soldiers from claims of jurisdiction under international law by the ICC and other foreign judicial authorities.

Persistent Barriers to U.S. Ratification

ICC supporters have called for the [Barack] Obama Administration to re-sign the Rome Statute, reverse protective measures secured during the Bush Administration . . . and fully embrace the ICC. Indeed, the Obama Administration may be considering some or all of those actions. However, the ICC's flaws advise caution and concern, particularly in how the ICC could affect national sovereignty and politically precarious situations around the globe.

Collateral Damage Could Result in ICC Charges Against the United States

U.S. officials do not fear genuine violations of international law; their true concern is that every tragedy of the U.S. war on terror will become the subject of a high-profile international criminal investigation. . . .

During the 1991 Gulf War . . . the United States used precision guided munitions to destroy the Al Firdos bunker in Baghdad [Iraq]. . . . After the bombing, however, Iraqi sources claimed that hundreds of civilians had been killed in the attack, including over 100 children. Unbeknownst to the United States, Iraq had housed the families of high-ranking civilians above the bunker either to provide them extra safety or to use as human shields. Public outrage against the attack—and charges of war crimes—immediately followed. . . .

Though collateral damage is inevitable, assessing its probability can be difficult. Moreover, incidents where the expected collateral damage exceeds military necessity could lead to actionable charges under the Rome Statute. But are judges and prosecutors of the ICC—who are not required to possess a military background or expertise in application of the laws of war—in the best position to evaluate these difficult determinations?

If the United States were a party to the ICC, every tragedy of collateral damage could potentially result in allegations of crimes against high-ranking U.S. officials.

> *W. Chadwick Austin and Antony Barone Kolene, "Who's Afraid of the Big Bad Wolf? The International Criminal Court as a Weapon of Asymmetric Warfare,"* Vanderbilt Journal of Transnational Law, *March 2006.*

When it decided to un-sign the Rome Statute, the Bush Administration voiced five concerns regarding the Rome Statute. These critical concerns have not been addressed.

The ICC's Unchecked Power. The U.S. system of government is based on the principle that power must be checked by other power or it will be abused and misused. With this in mind, the Founding Fathers divided the national government into three branches, giving each the means to influence and restrain excesses of the other branches. For instance, Congress confirms and can impeach federal judges and has the sole authority to authorize spending, the President nominates judges and can veto legislation, and the courts can nullify laws passed by Congress and overturn presidential actions if it judges them unconstitutional.

The ICC lacks robust checks on its authority, despite strong efforts by U.S. delegates to insert them during the treaty negotiations. The court is an independent treaty body. In theory, the states that have ratified the Rome Statute and accepted the court's authority control the ICC. In practice, the role of the Assembly of State Parties is limited. The judges themselves settle any dispute over the court's "judicial functions." The prosecutor can initiate an investigation on his own authority, and the ICC judges determine whether the investigation may proceed. The U.N. Security Council can delay an investigation for a year—a delay that can be renewed—but it cannot stop an investigation. . . .

The Challenges to the Security Council's Authority. The Rome Statute empowers the ICC to investigate, prosecute, and punish individuals for the as yet undefined crime of "aggression." This directly challenges the authority and prerogatives of the U.N. Security Council, which the U.N. Charter gives "primary responsibility for the maintenance of international peace and security" and which is the only U.N. institution empowered to determine when a nation has committed an act of aggression. Yet, the Rome Statute "empowers the court to decide on this matter and lets the prosecutor investigate and prosecute this undefined crime" free of any oversight from the Security Council.

A Threat to National Sovereignty. A bedrock principle of the international system is that treaties and the judgments and decisions of treaty organizations cannot be imposed on states without their consent. In certain circumstances, the ICC claims the authority to detain and try U.S. military personnel, U.S. officials, and other U.S. nationals even though the U.S. has not ratified the Rome Statute and has declared that it does not consider itself bound by its signature on the treaty. . . .

Protestations by ICC proponents that the court would seek such prosecutions only if a country is unwilling or unable to prosecute those accused of crimes within the court's jurisdiction—the principle of complementarity—are insufficient to alleviate sovereignty concerns. . . .

Erosion of Fundamental Elements of the U.N. Charter. The ICC's jurisdiction over war crimes, crimes against humanity, genocide, and aggression directly involves the court in fundamental issues traditionally reserved to sovereign states, such as when a state can lawfully use armed force to defend itself, its citizens, or its interests; how and to what extent armed force may be applied; and the point at which particular actions constitute serious crimes. Blurring the lines of authority and responsibility in these decisions has serious consequences. . . . The ability to project power must be protected, not only for America's own national security interests, but also for those individuals threatened by genocide and despotism who can only be protected through the use of force.

Complications to Military Cooperation Between the U.S. and Its Allies. The treaty creates an obligation to hand over U.S. nationals to the court, regardless of U.S. objections, absent a competing obligation such as that created through an Article 98 agreement. The United States has a unique role and responsibility in preserving international peace and security. At any given time, U.S. forces are located in approximately 100 nations around the world, standing ready to defend the interests of the U.S. and its allies, engaging in peacekeeping and humanitarian operations, conducting military exercises, or protecting U.S. interests through military intervention. The worldwide extension of U.S. armed forces is internationally unique. The U.S. must ensure that its soldiers and government officials are not exposed to politically motivated investigations and prosecutions.

Ongoing Causes for Concern

Supporters of U.S. ratification of the Rome Statute often dismiss these concerns as unjustified, disproved by the ICC's conduct during its first seven years in operation, or as insufficient to overcome the need for an international court to hold perpetrators of serious crimes to account. Considering the other options that exist or could be created to fill the ICC's role of holding perpetrators of war crimes, crimes against humanity, genocide, and aggression to account, the benefits from joining such a flawed institution do not justify the risks.

Furthermore, based on the ICC's record and the trend in international legal norms, they are being disingenuous in dismissing concerns about overpoliticization of the ICC, its impact on diplomatic initiatives and sovereign decisions on the use of force, its expansive claim of jurisdiction over the citizens of non-states parties, and incompatibility with U.S. legal norms and traditions. A number of specific risks are obvious.

Politicization of the Court. Unscrupulous individuals and groups and nations seeking to influence foreign policy and security decisions of other nations have and will continue to seek to misuse the ICC for politically motivated purposes. Without appropriate checks and balances to prevent its misuse, the ICC represents a dangerous temptation for those with political axes to grind. The prosecutor's *proprio motu* [on his own initiative] authority to initiate an investigation based solely on his own authority or on information provided by a government, a nongovernmental organization (NGO), or individuals is an open invitation for political manipulation. . . .

Disruption of Diplomatic Efforts. ICC decisions to pursue investigations and indictments can upset delicate diplomatic situations. Although the U.N. Security Council has been largely deadlocked over placing strong sanctions on the government of Sudan for its complicity in the terrible crimes in Darfur, it did pass a resolution in 2005 referring the situation in Darfur to the ICC. In summer 2008, the ICC announced that it would seek an indictment against Sudanese President Omar al-Bashir for his involvement in crimes committed in Darfur. On March 4, 2009, a warrant was issued for his arrest.

Issuing the arrest warrant for Bashir was certainly justified. His government has indisputably supported the janjaweed militias that have perpetrated massive human rights abuses that rise to the level of crimes against humanity. His complicity in the crimes demands that he be held to account. Regrettably, the decision to refer the case to the ICC and the subsequent decision to issue an arrest warrant for the sitting Sudanese head of state have aggravated the situation in Darfur and may put more innocent people at risk.

In response to his indictment, Bashir promptly expelled vital humanitarian NGOs from Sudan. Bashir may ultimately decide he has nothing to lose and increase his support of the janjaweed, encouraging them to escalate their attacks, even against aid workers and U.N. and AU peacekeepers serving in the African Union/U.N. Hybrid operation in Darfur (UNAMID). It could also undermine the 2005 peace agreement meant to reconcile the 20-year north-south civil war, which left more than 2 million dead.

Moreover, the decision to seek the arrest of Bashir, cheered by ICC supporters, may actually hurt the court in the long run. African countries, which would bear the most immediate consequences of a more chaotic Sudan, have called on the Security Council to defer the Bashir prosecution. Sudan's neighbors may be forced to choose between arresting Bashir, which could spark conflict with Sudan, or ignoring the court's arrest warrant. Indeed, all AU members except for Botswana announced in July 2009 that they would not cooperate with the ICC in this instance. South Africa subsequently announced that it would honor the ICC warrant in August 2009. Whether the AU decision will have broader ramifications for the court's relationship with African governments remains to be seen. Some African ICC parties have mentioned withdrawing from the Rome Statute.

The desire to see Bashir face justice for his role in the crimes committed in Darfur is understandable and should not be abandoned. However, premature efforts to bring Bashir to justice may be counterproductive. The priority in Sudan is to reduce the violence, stop the atrocities, restore peace and security, reconstitute refugees, and set the region on a path to avoid a return to conflict. This requires strong action by the AU and the international community, including economic and diplomatic sanctions designed to bring maximum pressure to bear on Bashir and his allies. It may require military intervention. Once this is achieved, justice can be pursued by the Sudanese themselves through their courts, through an ad hoc tribunal, or even through the ICC. . . .

The perpetrators of war crimes, genocide, and crimes against humanity should be held to account, but ICC investigation and arrest warrants cannot substitute for decisive action to stop the perpetrators and resolve such situations. Because the vast majority of the court's discretion lies within the Office of the Prosecutor, there is little opportunity to resolve disputes, conflicts, or sensitive political issues diplomatically after a case is brought to the ICC. . . .

The Undefined Crime of Aggression. It would be irresponsible for the U.S. to expose its military personnel and civilian officials to a court that has yet to define the very crimes over which it claims jurisdiction. Yet that is the situation the U.S. would face if it ratified the Rome Statute. The Statute includes the crime of aggression as one of its enumerated crimes, but the crime has yet to be defined, despite a special working group that has been debating the issue for more than five years.

For instance, some argue that any military action conducted without Security Council authorization violates international law and is, therefore, an act of aggression that could warrant an ICC indictment. The U.S. has been the aggressor in several recent military actions, including military invasions of the sovereign territories of Afghanistan and Iraq, albeit with the U.N. Security Council's blessing in the case of Afghanistan. U.S. forces bombed Serbia in 1999 and launched dozens of cruise missiles at targets in Afghanistan and the Sudan in 1998 without explicit Security Council authorization. While charges of aggression are unlikely to be brought against U.S. officials *ex post facto* [after the fact] for military actions in Iraq and elsewhere—certainly not for actions before July 2002 as limited by the Rome Statute—submitting to the jurisdiction of an international court that judges undefined crimes would be highly irresponsible and an open invitation to levy such charges against U.S. officials in future conflicts.

If the U.S. becomes an ICC party, every decision by the U.S. to use force, every civilian death resulting from U.S. military action and every allegedly abused detainee could conceivably give cause to America's enemies to file charges against U.S. soldiers and officials. . . .

Too Many Flaws in the ICC

While the International Criminal Court represents an admirable desire to hold war criminals accountable for their terrible crimes, the court is flawed notionally and operationally. The ICC has not overcome many of the problems plaguing the ad hoc tribunals established for Yugoslavia and Rwanda. It remains slow and inefficient. Worse, unlike ad hoc tribunals, it includes a drive to justify its budget and existence in perpetuity rather than simply completing a finite mission.

Its broad autonomy and jurisdiction invite politically motivated indictments. Its inflexibility can impede political resolution of problems, and its insulation from political considerations can complicate diplomatic efforts. Efforts to use the court to apply pressure to inherently political issues and supersede the foreign policy prerogatives of sovereign nations . . . undermine the court's credibility and threaten its future as a useful tool for holding accountable the perpetrators of genocide, war crimes, and crimes against humanity.

"The Obama Administration defends the human rights of LGBT people as part of our comprehensive human rights policy and as a priority of our foreign policy."

The United States Is a Leader in the Promotion of LGBT Human Rights

Hillary Rodham Clinton

In the following viewpoint, the US secretary of state argues that the pursuit of global human rights must include respect for and protection of lesbian, gay, bisexual, and transgender (LGBT) rights. In Switzerland, in 2011, she calls upon those assembled to view gay rights as human rights and to defend the integrity of all human beings regardless of their sexual orientation. She acknowledges that the United States has faced its own challenges in the treatment of homosexuals but that the country is now establishing policies under President Barack Obama to safeguard LGBT rights and support organizations around the world that promote equality for members of the LGBT community. Hillary Rodham Clinton became the US secretary of state in 2009 under the Obama administration.

Hillary Rodham Clinton, "Remarks in Recognition of International Human Rights Day," Geneva Switzerland, December 6, 2011. www.state.gov.

As you read, consider the following questions:

1. How does Clinton dismiss the notion that protecting LGBT rights is a luxury that only wealthy nations can afford?
2. What does Clinton believe happens when people fail to act in response to "denials and abuses" of human rights?
3. What is the purpose of the US-led Global Equality Fund, according to Clinton?

In the 63 years since the [UN Declaration of Human Rights] was adopted many nations have made great progress in making human rights a human reality. Step by step, barriers that once prevented people from enjoying the full measure of liberty, the full experience of dignity, and the full benefits of humanity have fallen away. In many places, racist laws have been repealed, legal and social practices that relegated women to second-class status have been abolished, the ability of religious minorities to practice their faith freely has been secured.

In most cases, this progress was not easily won. People fought and organized and campaigned in public squares and private spaces to change not only laws, but hearts and minds. And thanks to that work of generations, for millions of individuals whose lives were once narrowed by injustice, they are now able to live more freely and to participate more fully in the political, economic, and social lives of their communities.

There Is More Work to Do

Now there is still, as you all know, much more to be done to secure that commitment, that reality, and progress for all people. Today, I want to talk about the work we have left to do to protect one group of people whose human rights are still denied in too many parts of the world today. In many ways, they are an invisible minority. They are arrested, beaten, terrorized, even executed. Many are treated with contempt and violence by their fellow citizens while authorities empowered to protect them look the other way or, too often, even join in the abuse. They are denied opportunities to work and learn, driven from their homes and countries, and forced to suppress or deny who they are to protect themselves from harm.

I am talking about gay, lesbian, bisexual, and transgender people, human beings born free and given bestowed equality and dignity, who have a right to claim that, which is now one of the remaining human rights challenges of our time. I speak about this subject knowing that my own country's record on human rights for gay people is far from perfect. Until 2003, it was still a crime in parts of our country. Many LGBT Americans have endured violence and harassment in their own lives, and for some, including many young people bullying and exclusion are daily experiences. So we, like all nations, have more work to do to protect human rights at home.

Now, raising this issue, I know, is sensitive for many people and that the obstacles standing in the way of protecting the human rights of LGBT people rest on deeply held personal, political, cultural, and religious beliefs. So I come here before you with respect, understanding, and humility. Even though progress on this front is not easy, we cannot delay acting. So in that spirit, I want to talk about the difficult and important issues we must address together to reach a global consensus that recognizes the human rights of LGBT citizens everywhere.

Gay Rights Are Human Rights

The first issue goes to the heart of the matter. Some have suggested that gay rights and human rights are separate and distinct; but, in fact, they are one and the same. Now, of course, 60 years ago, the governments that drafted and passed the Universal Declaration of Human Rights were not thinking about how it applied to the LGBT community. They also weren't thinking about how it applied to indigenous people or children or people with disabilities or other marginalized groups. Yet in the past 60 years, we have come to recognize that members of these groups are entitled to the full measure of dignity and rights, because, like all people, they share a common humanity.

This recognition did not occur all at once. It evolved over time. And as it did, we understood that we were honoring rights that people always had, rather than creating new or special rights for them. Like being a woman, like being a racial, religious, tribal, or ethnic minority, being LGBT does not make you less human. And that is why gay rights are human rights, and human rights are gay rights.

It is a violation of human rights when people are beaten or killed because of their sexual orientation, or because they do not conform to cultural norms about how men and women should look or behave. It is a violation of human rights when governments declare it illegal to be gay, or allow those who harm gay people to go unpunished. It is a violation of human rights when lesbian or transgendered women are subjected to so-called corrective rape, or forcibly subjected to hormone treatments, or when people are murdered after public calls for violence toward gays, or when they are forced to flee their nations and seek asylum in other lands to save their lives. And it is a violation of human rights when life-saving care is withheld from people because they are gay, or equal access to justice is denied to people because they are gay, or public spaces are out of bounds to people because they are gay. No matter what we look like, where we come from, or who we are, we are all equally entitled to our human rights and dignity.

Homosexuality Is Not a Product of Western Culture

The second issue is a question of whether homosexuality arises from a particular part of the world. Some seem to believe it is a Western phenomenon, and therefore people outside the West have grounds to reject it. Well, in reality, gay people are born into and belong to every society in the world. They are all ages, all races, all faiths; they are doctors and teachers, farmers and bankers, soldiers and athletes; and whether we know it, or whether we acknowledge it, they are our family, our friends, and our neighbors.

Being gay is not a Western invention; it is a human reality. And protecting the human rights of all people, gay or straight, is not something that only Western governments do. South Africa's constitution, written in the aftermath of Apartheid [the legal separation of whites and blacks in that country], protects the equality of all citizens, including gay people. In Colombia and Argentina, the rights of gays are also legally protected. In Nepal, the supreme court has ruled that equal rights apply to LGBT citizens. The Government of Mongolia has committed to pursue new legislation that will tackle anti-gay discrimination.

Now, some worry that protecting the human rights of the LGBT community is a luxury that only wealthy nations can afford. But in fact, in all countries, there are costs to not protecting these rights, in both gay and straight lives lost to disease and violence, and the silencing of voices and views that would strengthen communities, in ideas never pursued by entrepreneurs who happen to be gay. Costs are incurred whenever any group is treated as lesser or the other, whether they are women, racial, or religious minorities, or the LGBT. Former President Mogae of Botswana pointed out recently that for as long as LGBT people are kept in the shadows, there cannot be an effective public health program to tackle HIV and AIDS. Well, that holds true for other challenges as well.

Religion Does Not Justify Violating Human Rights

The third, and perhaps most challenging, issue arises when people cite religious or cultural values as a reason to violate or not to protect the human rights of LGBT citizens. This is not unlike the justification offered for violent practices towards women like honor killings, widow burning, or female genital mutilation.

Some people still defend those practices as part of a cultural tradition. But violence toward women isn't cultural; it's criminal. Likewise with slavery, what was once justified as sanctioned by God is now properly reviled as an unconscionable violation of human rights.

In each of these cases, we came to learn that no practice or tradition trumps the human rights that belong to all of us. And this holds true for inflicting violence on LGBT people, criminalizing their status or behavior, expelling them from their families and communities, or tacitly or explicitly accepting their killing.

Of course, it bears noting that rarely are cultural and religious traditions and teachings actually in conflict with the protection of human rights. Indeed, our religion and our culture are sources of compassion and inspiration toward our fellow human beings. It was not only those who've justified slavery who leaned on religion, it was also those who sought to abolish it. And let us keep in mind that our commitments to protect the freedom of religion and to defend the dignity of LGBT people emanate from a common source. For many of us, religious belief and practice is a vital source of meaning and identity, and fundamental to who we are as people. And likewise, for most of us, the bonds of love and family that we forge are also vital sources of meaning and identity. And caring for others is an expression of what it means to be fully human. It is because the human experience is universal that human rights are universal and cut across all religions and cultures.

Progress Through Dialogue and a Respect for Equality

The fourth issue is what history teaches us about how we make progress towards rights for all. Progress starts with honest discussion. Now, there are some who say and believe that all gay people are pedophiles, that homosexuality is a disease that can be caught or cured, or that gays recruit others to become gay. Well, these notions are simply not true. They are also unlikely to disappear if those who promote or accept them are dismissed out of hand rather than invited to share their fears and concerns. No one has ever abandoned a belief because he was forced to do so.

Universal human rights include freedom of expression and freedom of belief, even if our words or beliefs denigrate the humanity of others. Yet, while we are each free to believe whatever we choose, we cannot do whatever we choose, not in a world where we protect the human rights of all.

Reaching understanding of these issues takes more than speech. It does take a conversation. In fact, it takes a constellation of conversations in places big and small. And it takes a willingness to see stark differences in belief as a reason to begin the conversation, not to avoid it.

But progress comes from changes in laws. In many places, including my own country, legal protections have preceded, not followed, broader recognition of rights. Laws have a teaching effect. Laws that discriminate validate other kinds of discrimination. Laws that require equal protections reinforce the moral imperative of equality. And practically speaking, it is often the case that laws must change before fears about change dissipate.

Many in my country thought that President [Harry S.] Truman was making a grave error when he ordered the racial desegregation of our military. They argued that it would undermine unit cohesion. And it wasn't until he went ahead and did it that we saw how it strengthened our social fabric in ways even the supporters of the policy could not foresee. Likewise, some worried in my country that the repeal of "Don't Ask, Don't Tell" [policy that stipulated homosexual soldiers should not reveal their sexual orientation during military service] would have a negative effect on our armed forces. Now, the Marine Corps Commandant, who was one of the strongest voices against the repeal, says that his concerns were unfounded and that the Marines have embraced the change.

Finally, progress comes from being willing to walk a mile in someone else's shoes. We need to ask ourselves, "How would it feel if it were a crime to love the person I love? How would it feel

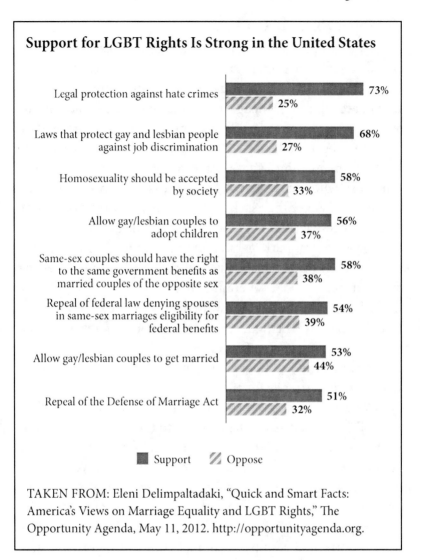

Support for LGBT Rights Is Strong in the United States

Legal protection against hate crimes — 73% / 25%

Laws that protect gay and lesbian people against job discrimination — 68% / 27%

Homosexuality should be accepted by society — 58% / 33%

Allow gay/lesbian couples to adopt children — 56% / 37%

Same-sex couples should have the right to the same government benefits as married couples of the opposite sex — 58% / 38%

Repeal of federal law denying spouses in same-sex marriages eligibility for federal benefits — 54% / 39%

Allow gay/lesbian couples to get married — 53% / 44%

Repeal of the Defense of Marriage Act — 51% / 32%

■ Support ▨ Oppose

TAKEN FROM: Eleni Delimpaltadaki, "Quick and Smart Facts: America's Views on Marriage Equality and LGBT Rights," The Opportunity Agenda, May 11, 2012. http://opportunityagenda.org.

to be discriminated against for something about myself that I cannot change?" This challenge applies to all of us as we reflect upon deeply held beliefs, as we work to embrace tolerance and respect for the dignity of all persons, and as we engage humbly with those with whom we disagree in the hope of creating greater understanding.

Taking a United Stand

A fifth and final question is how we do our part to bring the world to embrace human rights for all people including LGBT people. Yes, LGBT people must help lead this effort, as so many of you are. Their knowledge and experiences are invaluable and their courage inspirational. We know the names of brave LGBT activists who have literally given their lives for this cause, and there are many more whose names we will never know. But often those who are denied rights are least empowered to bring about the changes they seek. Acting alone, minorities can never achieve the majorities necessary for political change.

So when any part of humanity is sidelined, the rest of us cannot sit on the sidelines. Every time a barrier to progress has fallen, it has taken a cooperative effort from those on both sides of the barrier. In the fight for women's rights, the support of men remains crucial. The fight for racial equality has relied on contributions from people of all races. Combating Islamaphobia or anti-Semitism is a task for people of all faiths. And the same is true with this struggle for equality.

Conversely, when we see denials and abuses of human rights and fail to act, that sends the message to those deniers and abusers that they won't suffer any consequences for their actions, and so they carry on. But when we do act, we send a powerful moral message. Right here in Geneva, the international community acted this year to strengthen a global consensus around the human rights of LGBT people. At the Human Rights Council in March [2011], 85 countries from all regions supported a statement calling for an end to criminalization and violence against people because of their sexual orientation and gender identity.

At the following session of the Council in June, South Africa took the lead on a resolution about violence against LGBT people. The delegation from South Africa spoke eloquently about their own experience and struggle for human equality and its indivisibility. When the measure passed, it became the first-ever UN resolution recognizing the human rights of gay people worldwide. In the Organization of American States this year, the Inter-American Commission on Human Rights created a unit on the rights of LGBT people, a step toward what we hope will be the creation of a special rapporteur.

Now, we must go further and work here and in every region of the world to galvanize more support for the human rights of the LGBT community. To the leaders of those countries where people are jailed, beaten, or executed for being gay, I ask you to consider this: Leadership, by definition, means being out in front of your people when it is called for. It means standing up for the dignity of all your citizens and persuading your people to do the same. It also means ensuring that all citizens are treated as equals under your laws, because let me be clear—I am not saying that gay people can't or don't commit crimes. They can and they do, just like straight people. And when they do, they should be held accountable, but it should never be a crime to be gay.

And to people of all nations, I say supporting human rights is your responsibility too. The lives of gay people are shaped not only by laws, but by the treatment they receive every day from their families, from their neighbors. Eleanor Roosevelt, who did so much to advance human rights worldwide, said that these rights begin in the small places close to home—the streets where people live, the schools they attend, the factories, farms, and offices where they work. These places are your domain. The actions you take, the ideals that you advocate, can determine whether human rights flourish where you are.

The United States' Commitment to LGBT Rights

And finally, to LGBT men and women worldwide, let me say this: Wherever you live and whatever the circumstances of your life, whether you are connected to a network of support or feel isolated and vulnerable, please know that you are not alone. People around the globe are working hard to support you and to bring an end to the injustices and dangers you face. That is certainly true for my country. And you have an ally in the United States of America and you have millions of friends among the American people.

The [Barack] Obama Administration defends the human rights of LGBT people as part of our comprehensive human rights policy and as a priority of our foreign policy. In our embassies, our diplomats are raising concerns about specific cases and laws, and working with a range of partners to strengthen human rights protections for all. In Washington, we have created a task force at the State Department to support and coordinate this work. And in the coming months, we will provide every embassy with a toolkit to help improve their efforts. And we have created a program that offers emergency support to defenders of human rights for LGBT people.

This morning, back in Washington, President Obama put into place the first U.S. Government strategy dedicated to combating human rights abuses against LGBT persons abroad. Building on efforts already underway at the State Department and across the government, the President has directed all U.S. Government agencies engaged overseas to combat the criminalization of LGBT status and conduct, to enhance efforts to protect vulnerable LGBT refugees and asylum seekers, to ensure that our foreign assistance promotes the protection of LGBT rights, to enlist international organizations in the fight against discrimination, and to respond swiftly to abuses against LGBT persons.

I am also pleased to announce that we are launching a new Global Equality Fund that will support the work of civil society organizations working on these issues around the world. This fund will help them record facts so they can target their advocacy, learn how to use the law as a tool, manage their budgets, train their staffs, and forge partnerships with women's organizations and other human rights groups. We have committed more than $3 million to start this fund, and we have hope that others will join us in supporting it.

Evidence of Global Change

The women and men who advocate for human rights for the LGBT community in hostile places, some of whom are here today with us, are brave and dedicated, and deserve all the help we can give them. We know the road ahead will not be easy. A great deal of work lies before us. But many of us have seen firsthand how quickly change can come. In our lifetimes, attitudes toward gay people in many places have been transformed. Many people, including myself, have experienced a deepening of our own convictions on this topic over the years, as we have devoted more thought to it, engaged in dialogues and debates, and established personal and professional relationships with people who are gay.

This evolution is evident in many places. To highlight one example, the Delhi High Court decriminalized homosexuality in India two years ago, writing, and I quote, "If there is one tenet that can be said to be an underlying theme of the Indian constitution, it is inclusiveness." There is little doubt in my mind that support for LGBT human rights will continue to climb. Because for many young people, this is simple: All people deserve to be treated with dignity and have their human rights respected, no matter who they are or whom they love.

There is a phrase that people in the United States invoke when urging others to support human rights: "Be on the right side of history." The story of the United States is the story of a nation that has repeatedly grappled with intolerance and inequality. We fought a brutal civil war over slavery. People from coast to coast joined in campaigns to recognize the rights of women, indigenous peoples, racial minorities, children, people with disabilities, immigrants, workers, and on and on. And the march toward equality and justice has continued. Those who advocate for expanding the circle of human rights were and are on the right side of history, and history honors them. Those who tried to constrict human rights were wrong, and history reflects that as well.

I know that the thoughts I've shared today involve questions on which opinions are still evolving. As it has happened so many times before, opinion will converge once again with the truth, the immutable truth, that all persons are created free and equal in dignity and rights. We are called once more to make real the words of the Universal Declaration. Let us answer that call. Let us be on the right side of history, for our people, our nations, and future generations, whose lives will be shaped by the work we do today. I come before you with great hope and confidence that no matter how long the road ahead, we will travel it successfully together.

> "The United States and many of our
> elected officials lag far behind the
> public when it comes to granting rights
> for sexual minorities."

The Mythology of a Human Rights Leader: How the United States Has Failed Sexual Minorities at Home and Abroad

Stacey L. Sobel*

In the following viewpoint, an attorney decries the lack of progress of lesbian, gay, bisexual, and transgender (LGBT) human rights in the United States. According to the author, the United States touts itself as a champion of human rights when, in fact, it has fallen behind other nations in protecting LGBT rights and has tolerated the restriction of certain rights, such as the right to marry. Stacey Sobel, an attorney and a lecturer of law at the University of Pennsylvania, is an advocate on issues related to the LGBT community.

As you read, consider the following questions:

1. Who does Sobel indict for wanting to dismiss LGBT rights as "special rights"?

Stacey L. Sobel, "The Mythology of a Human Rights Leader: How the United States Has Failed Sexual Minorities at Home and Abroad," *Harvard Human Rights Journal*, vol. 21, no. 2, Summer 2008, pp. 197–205. Copyright © 2008 by the Harvard Human Rights Journal. All rights reserved. Reproduced by permission.

2. What is DOMA, and how does it reflect the United States' unwillingness to promote LGBT rights, according to Sobel?

3. How many military personnel were discharged under the "Don't Ask, Don't Tell" policy, according to Sobel?

Most Americans develop a belief that the United States serves as a human rights leader and role model. This belief is instilled in us through our families, teachers, the media, and the United States government, among others. Similar to other types of mythology, it is based partially in fact and it is influenced by the way people would prefer to see the world. And like many types of mythology, it is not always true.

The United States is typically held to a higher human rights standard than other countries. It is not enough for the United States *to follow* other countries; the United States is expected *to lead* the charge. When it does not lead, other nations may lack the incentive to meet the highest human rights standards because merely meeting our level would be sufficient. They will point to the United States and say, "if it is good enough for them, it is good enough for us."

This human rights mythology has been fostered by the concept that greater opportunities for equality exist in the United States. Millions of people came to this country because here they were able to achieve levels of financial and social prosperity that were unattainable in other nations. These immigrants believed in proverbs such as "if you work hard you can do anything in America," and "it doesn't matter who you are or where you come from in order to succeed in the United States."

Our mythology is also derived from a number of legal premises, including the Declaration of Independence's avowal that all men are created equal[1] and the equal protection[2] and due process[3] clauses of the United States Constitution. While most people want to believe that these tenets will always be applied fairly, they, of course, are not.

The role of the United States as a human rights leader has evolved from our early isolationist policies to our increasing involvement in international activities during the twentieth century. The United States was seen as a hero to many for its involvement in both world wars, and the pictures of U.S. soldiers and tanks riding into European towns or rescuing people from concentration camps etched this new status into many peoples' minds.

Similarly, our involvement in the United Nations and other peacekeeping actions over the last fifty years,[4] and our insistence on improving human rights as a prerequisite to our support of nations like China,[5] have helped to raise our stature as a human rights leader.

Even though the mythology exists, there are many instances where the United States has not been a human rights leader. The United States has a history of discrimination that reaches back as far as our belief that America is the land of opportunity. There was a time when it was perfectly acceptable to openly discriminate against Irish, Italian, Chinese, Jewish, African American, and other groups in our country. While many of the same teachers who taught us about American success stories also taught us about the help wanted signs that stated "No_____ Need Apply," the mythology of our country as a human rights leader usually prevailed. We would rather remember the hope that brought Japanese people to the United States than the internment camps in which they were held during World War II.

As a young child, I was enthralled with American history and I fully bought into the mythology of the United States as a champion of the underdog and the downtrodden. As an adult, the reality has proved disappointing. I still see the United States participating in international human rights efforts, but I feel as though the United States has failed people who are sexual minorities.[6] It has failed me as a lesbian, a partner, and a mother. It has failed to grant me the same human rights and the same equality that I was taught to expect from the United States.

Human Rights and Sexual Minorities

Many people incorrectly assume that the United States' dedication to human rights and equality extends to all disadvantaged groups. The United States has made advancements in human rights domestically and internationally in many areas, but it continues to fail on the issue of human rights for lesbian, gay, bisexual, and transgender ("LGBT") individuals.

"[R]ecognition of the inherent dignity and of the equal and inalienable rights of all members of the human family" is the framework of the human rights movement.[7] Human rights include the ability to work and provide the necessities of life for yourself and your family. These are not "special rights," as they are often defined by conservatives who oppose LGBT equality,[8] but the most basic ability of individuals to take care of themselves. As long as bias and prejudice against LGBT people exists without the benefit of legal protections, this basic level of human rights will be difficult for some people to attain.

The United States and many of our elected officials lag far behind the public when it comes to granting rights for sexual minorities. Only twenty states have non-discrimination laws prohibiting some level of discrimination against LGBT people,[9] and no federal law prohibits this type of discrimination despite repeated attempts to pass the Employment Non-Discrimination Act[10] in the United States Congress since 1994.

The lack of legislative support for LGBT-inclusive non-discrimination laws is surprising in light of the fact that eighty-nine percent of Americans believe that gay or lesbian people should have equal rights in terms of job opportunities.[11] This reluctance or unwillingness to pursue legislation that would protect LGBT people is often based on limited, but very vocal, opposition.

On the international level, other countries and regional bodies are leading the way against LGBT discrimination. In 2000, the Council of the European Union, for example, passed a resolution declaring that direct or indirect employment discrimination based on sexual orientation was prohibited.[12] Unlike countries in the European Union, the United States does not have external legal or political influences to move it towards prohibiting LGBT discrimination. In fact, the United States often refuses to acknowledge basic international law, and as a result, the advances in other parts of the world have little impact domestically. This bias was demonstrated in Justice Scalia's dissenting opinion in *Lawrence v. Texas*,[13] in which he decried the majority opinion's discussion of international law as it related to LGBT people and sodomy laws.[14]

It is disappointing that the U.S. government and some of its judges are unwilling to acknowledge the human rights progress being made by other nations. Just because an idea does not originate in the United States does not make that idea a foreign fad without basis or merit.[15] Since the federal government has not granted non-discrimination protections for LGBT people, progress will have to continue at the state level in order to create "home grown" support for recognizing the human rights of sexual minorities in the United States.

Relationship Recognition for Same-Sex Couples

Some of the greatest disparities between human rights advances abroad and in the United States can be seen in relationship recognition issues. When it comes to relationship recognition rights, the United States is being left behind by most European nations and other countries that are considered to be leaders in this emerging human rights area.

Countries such as Canada, the Netherlands, Belgium, Spain and South Africa are leading the way for relationship recognition by granting marriage equality to same-sex couples.[16] Other nations such as Denmark, Finland, France, Germany, Iceland, Israel, Norway, Portugal, Sweden, Switzerland, the United Kingdom and Uruguay do not grant the legal status of marriage to same-sex couples, but they grant some level of relationship recognition providing all or some of the rights often associated with civil marriage.[17]

International organizations have also ruled that denying relationship recognition rights violates their tenets. For example, the United Nations' Human Rights Committee ruled that Australia, in denying pension benefits to the surviving same-sex partner of a war veteran, violated anti-discrimination principles codified in the International Covenant on Civil and Political Rights.[18]

The countries and international bodies cited above are at the vanguard of these human rights developments. Some nations are reluctantly joining them or being forced to join them by human rights directives outside their countries. Even countries such as Spain, where religious influence is strong, are enacting laws recognizing same-sex couples.[19]

At the same time as the above countries are granting relationship recognition rights to sexual minorities, other parts of the world face a very different reality. In much of the world, it is still against the law for people to engage in same-sex sexual activities,[20] and legal relationship recognition is unattainable for the foreseeable future. In some nations, lesbian and gay people are still routinely thrown in jail or sentenced to death because of their sexual orientation or for engaging in same-sex sexual activities or relationships.[21] And other countries such as Nigeria are proposing even stricter laws against LGBT people.[22]

The U.S. government is not acting as a human rights leader in the area of relationship recognition. In fact, it is bucking the trend of most other countries that are typically at the forefront of human rights. The United States not only lacks a national law granting any rights to same-sex couples, it has prevented same-sex couples from receiving federally recognized marriages by passing the Defense of Marriage Act ("DOMA") in 1996. [23] DOMA defines marriage as "only a legal union between one man and one woman as husband and wife, and the word 'spouse' refers only to a person of the opposite sex who is a husband or a wife."[24] DOMA not only limits the federal recognition of marriage to a man and a woman, but it further states that:

No State, territory, or possession of the United States, or Indian tribe, shall be required to give effect to any public act, record, or judicial proceeding of any other State, territory, possession, or tribe respecting a relationship between persons of the same sex that is treated as a marriage under the laws of such other State, territory, possession, or tribe, or a right or claim arising from such relationship.[25]

The DOMA law is an example of the backlash that takes place whenever a step forward in the area of relationship recognition occurs in this country. Congress passed the federal law in response to a Hawaii Supreme Court decision holding that denying marriage rights to same-sex couples implicated equal protection concerns.[26] Shortly after the federal law was passed, state legislatures throughout the country began passing "mini-DOMA" laws prohibiting marriage equality in their states and, in some cases, "super-DOMA" laws, preventing any legal recognition of unmarried couples.[27] Additional states passed mini-DOMA laws[28] after Vermont began offering civil unions at the behest of its Supreme Court in 1999.[29] Currently, thirty-eight states have DOMA laws.[30]

Another round of backlash legislation[31] began after the Massachusetts Supreme Court ruled that same-sex couples must be granted the same rights and responsibilities of marriage as heterosexual couples.[32] Some members of the United States Senate and House of Representatives have introduced "Federal Marriage Amendments" to prohibit relationship recognition for same-sex couples in the U.S. Constitution.[33] While the attempts to amend the U.S. Constitution in the last few years have failed, many states have successfully amended their state constitutions to prohibit marriage equality, and some states have gone even further by also prohibiting relationship recognition of any kind for unmarried couples.[34]

As these efforts to strip LGBT people of basic human rights have continued, gradually more states are recognizing same-sex relationships in a variety of forms. Massachusetts is still the only state with full marriage equality, but six states now offer civil unions or some other legal status granting all of the rights and responsibilities of marriage, and three additional states and the District of Columbia have more limited recognition rights for same-sex couples.[35]

It has been only five years since sodomy laws were held unconstitutional in the United States. Even though most states had stricken their sodomy laws by the time *Lawrence v. Texas* was decided, the Supreme Court's previous decision that there was no constitutionally protected right to homosexual sodomy[36] influenced relationship recognition laws around the country. After all, it is harder to argue for relationship recognition and human rights when the Supreme Court has ruled that it is permissible to treat sexual minorities like criminals.

The limited human rights advancements for sexual minorities in the United States largely stem from the increased visibility of LGBT people in the last forty years. As the number of LGBT people "coming out" has risen, there has been a corresponding increase in the acceptance of sexual minorities and demands to address the legal needs of same-sex couples.

The progress and simultaneous regression of relationship recognition for same-sex couples in the United States demonstrates the evolving nature of this issue. As the U.S. struggles with this issue in state and federal courts and legislatures, other countries are paving the way by granting relationship recognition to same-sex couples.

Human Rights and "Don't Ask, Don't Tell"

The United States' ban against openly lesbian, gay, and bisexual service members sets it apart from many of its peer countries. While American service members are often asked to defend the human rights of individuals abroad, they lack some of the basic human rights that others enjoy. These Americans are forced to lie and hide their sexual orientation every day in order to keep their jobs or avoid harassment, assault, or in some cases death.

The current U.S. law concerning lesbian, gay, and bisexual service members in the military was passed in 1993.[37] What began as a compromise between strong-willed military and congressional leaders and a president who made a campaign promise to end the code of silence in the armed services has been a failure. Like many compromises, "Don't Ask, Don't Tell" has not met the objectives of either side in the debate. More than 10,000 service members have been discharged under the law since its implementation[38] and critical, skilled jobs remain vacant when the country is at war.[39]

Ironically, while "Don't Ask, Don't Tell" continues to silence United States service men and women, our forces are serving next to openly lesbian, gay, and bisexual members of other countries' militaries. Twenty-two other nations with troops serving in Iraq allow openly lesbian, gay, and bisexual service members in their militaries.[40] Those individuals are working with United States service members and there have been no reports that their presence negatively impacts our troops' ability to serve.

When defending the United States' discriminatory policy in the past, military experts would point to the fact that England had a similar law on the books.[41] In 2000, Britain began allowing lesbian, gay, and bisexual service members to serve openly after the European Court of Human Rights ruled that its military ban violated the European Convention on Human Rights.[42] British military leaders predicted all types of problems with implementing the new law. None occurred.[43]

Some people may believe that "Don't Ask, Don't Tell" has a limited impact on LGBT people in the United States. Its impact, however, is significant because the federal government has set the standard that it is permissible to proactively discriminate against people based upon their sexual orientation. As long as it remains the law, LGBT rights opponents will rely on "Don't Ask, Don't Tell" to discriminate in other areas, such as arguing that it is also permissible for private employers to discriminate against LGBT people. The United States cannot claim to be a true human rights leader until its soldiers, sailors, airmen and marines are able to do their jobs without fear of reprisal for being lesbian, gay, or bisexual.

Conclusion

As an attorney who works for equal rights in this country, it is disappointing to see state and federal laws ignoring or depriving the human rights of the people I serve. Since the framework for equality exists for LGBT people in the United States, I believe that sooner, rather than later, we will have the same rights, benefits and protections as others in our country. I also see a day when the United States will live up to its mythology as a human rights leader—a day when it joins other nations working to legally recognize the rights of sexual minorities internationally. Until that time, the United States' lack of leadership will prevent the evolution of human rights for sexual minorities in many other parts of the world because other countries will justify their own human rights failures by the minimal standards set in this country.

Notes

* Executive director of Equality Advocates Pennsylvania, Lecturer of Law at the University of Pennsylvania Law School where she teaches Sexual Orientation, Gender Identity and the Law.
1. THE DECLARATION OF INDEPENDENCE para. 2 (U.S. 1776).
2. U.S. CONST. amend. XIV, §1.
3. U.S. CONST. amend. V, §1; *id.* amend. XIV, §1
4. "Currently, the United States provides military observers and UN police for eight peacekeeping missions: Liberia (UNMIL), the Democratic Republic of the Congo (MONUC), Sudan (UNMIS), Ethiopia/Eritrea (UNMEE), Haiti (MINUSTAH), Timor-Leste (UNMIT), the Middle East (UNTSO), and Kosovo (UNMIK)." Bureau of Int'l Org. Affairs, Dep't of State, U.S. Support for UN Peacekeeping, UN Sanctions Committees, and UN Counter-terrorism Efforts, http://www.state.gov/p/io/pkpg/ (last visited January 24, 2008).
5. See Bureau of East Asian and Pacific Affairs, Dep't of State, Fact Sheet: Increased Respect for Human Rights in China a U.S. Priority, http://usinfo.state.gov/eap /Archive/2006/Apr/19-741526.html (last visited Apr. 21, 2008).

6. Sexual minorities are individuals with sexual orientations and gender identities that do not con-form with the majority. This includes people who are lesbian, gay, bisexual, or transgender.

7. Universal Declaration of Human Rights, G.A. Res. 217A, at 71, U.N. GAOR, 3d Sess., 1stplen. mtg., U.N. Doc A/810 (Dec. 12, 1948).

8. See, e.g., Concerned Women for America, Homosexual Special Rights, http://www .cwfa.org/arti-cledisplay.asp?id=932&department=CWA&categoryid=family (last visited Apr. 21, 2008); Family Research Council, Oppose Special Rights Bill for Homosexual Conduct, http://capwiz.com/frc/callalert/index.tt?alertid=10524841 (last visited Jan. 24, 2008).

9. California, Colorado, Connecticut, Hawaii, Illinois, Iowa, Maine, Maryland, Massachusetts, Minnesota, Nevada, New Hampshire, New Jersey, New Mexico, New York, Oregon, Rhode Island, Vermont, Washington, Wisconsin, and the District of Columbia have laws protecting gay, lesbian, and bisexual people from discrimination. Seven of these states prohibit discrimination only on the basis of sexual orientation and the remaining thirteen states cover sexual orientation and gender identity. These laws usually prohibit discrimination in the areas of employment, housing and public accommodations. National Gay and Lesbian Task Force, Issue Map: State Non-Discrimination Laws in the U.S. (Jan. 8, 2008), http://www.thetaskforce.org/downloads /reports/issue_maps/non_discrimination_01_08_color.pdf (last visited Apr. 21, 2008).

10. H.R. 3685, 110th Cong. (1st Sess., 2007). This version of the legislation prohibited sexual orientation discrimination, but did not include gender identity discrimination.

11. Lydia Saad, *Tolerance of Gay Rights at High-Water Mark*, GALLUP NEWS SERVICE, May 29, 2007, available at http://www.gallup.com/poll/27694/Tolerance-Gay-Rights -HighWater-Mark.aspx.

12. Council Directive 2000/78, Establishing a General Framework for Equal Treatment in Employment and Occupation, 2000 O.J. (L 303) 16 (EC), available at http://ec.europa .eu/employ-ment_social/news/2001/jul/directive78ec_en.pdf.

13. 539 U.S. 558, 586-605 (2003) (Scalia, J., dissenting).

14. In his dissent, Justice Scalia affirmed that constitutional entitlements do not "spring into existence . . . because *foreign nations* decriminalize conduct." *Id.* at 598.

15. Justice Scalia further states in *Lawrence* that "this Court . . . should not impose foreign moods, fads, or fashions on Americans." *Id.* (quoting Foster v. Florida, 537 U.S. 990, 990 (2002) (Thomas, J., concurring in denial of certiorari)).

16. See Hope Lozano-Bielat & David Masci, *Same-Sex Marriage: Redefining Legal Unions Around the World*, PEW RESEARCH CENTER (July 11, 2007), available at http:// pewresearch.org/pubs/541/gay-marriage.

17. Marriage Equality USA, Get the Facts on Marriage, http://www.marriageequality.org /meusa/facts.shtml?marriage-status (last visited Apr. 17, 2008).

18. Young v. Australia, U.N. Human Rights Comm., Communication No. 941/2000, U.N. Doc. CCPR/C/78/D/941/2000 (2003).

19. See Ley 13/2005, de 1 de julio, por la que se modifica el C´odigo Civil en material de derecho acontraer matrimonio (Law of July 1 modifying the Civil Code in the area of contracting marriage) (B.O.E. 2005, 157), available at http://www.unex.es/unex /gobierno/direccion/vicedoc/archivos/ficheros/igualdad/legislacion/ley13_2005.pdf.

20. See Sodomy Laws Around the World, http://www.sodomylaws.org (last visited Jan. 24, 2008).

21. See, e.g., Dominic Kennedy, *Gays Should Be Hanged, Says Minister*, TIMES (London), Nov. 13, 2007, at 36 (discussing reported executions of gays in Iran); Lydia Polgreen,

Nigerian Anglicans Seeing Gay Challenge to Orthodoxy, N.Y. TIMES, Dec. 18, 2005, §1, at 3 (reporting that gay men and lesbians in Nigeria are often arrested and jailed).

22. A Nigerian law was proposed that may have made it illegal for any LGBT person to eat or socialize with someone of the same sex. See *New Law and Old Prejudices Threaten Nigeria's Gay Community*, INT'L HERALD TRIB., Dec. 11, 2006, available at http://www.iht.com/articles/ap/2006/12/11/africa/AF_FEA_GEN_Nigerian_and_Gay.php.

23. Defense of Marriage Act, 1 U.S.C. §7, 28 U.S.C. §1738C (1996).

24. 1 U.S.C. §7.

25. 28 U.S.C. §1738C.

26. See Baehr v. Lewin, 852 P.2d 44 (Haw. 1993); H.R. REP. NO. 104–664, at 2 (1996) (describing DOMA as a response to *Baehr*).

27. From 1996 to 1998, Arizona, Delaware, Georgia, Idaho, Illinois, Kansas, Michigan, Missouri, North Carolina, Oklahoma, Pennsylvania, South Carolina, South Dakota, Tennessee, Arkansas, Indiana, Maine, Minnesota, Mississippi, North Dakota, Virginia, Alabama, Hawaii, Iowa, Kentucky and Washington passed mini-DOMA laws. Alaska, Florida and Montana passed super-DOMA laws. National Gay and Lesbian Task Force, Issue Map: Anti-Gay Marriage Measures in the U.S. (Sept. 25, 2007), http://thetaskforce.org/downloads/reports/issue_maps/GayMarriage_09_25_07.pdf [hereinafter Anti-Gay Marriage Measures] (last visited Apr. 21, 2008).

28. Louisiana, California, Colorado, West Virginia and Missouri passed mini-DOMA laws from 1999 through 2002. *Id.*

29. See Baker v. Vermont, 744 A.2d 864 (Vt. 1999).

30. Anti-Gay Marriage Measures, *supra* note 27. R

31. New Hampshire passed a mini-DOMA law and Texas, Virginia and Ohio passed super-DOMA laws in 2003 and 2004. *Id.*

32. See Goodridge v. Dep't of Pub. Health, 798 N.E.2d 941 (Mass. 2003).

33. Eleven such amendments to the U.S. Constitution have been offered in the U.S. House or Senate since 2004. The only pending amendment is H.R.J. Res. 22, 110th Cong. (1st Sess. 2007).

34. Twenty-six states now have constitutional provisions prohibiting marriage equality or more. Twenty-three of these were passed after *Goodridge*, including Missouri, Mississippi, Montana, Oregon, Louisiana, Arkansas, Georgia, Kentucky, Michigan, North Dakota, Ohio, Oklahoma, Utah, Kansas, Texas, Colorado, Tennessee, Alabama, Idaho, South Carolina, South Dakota, Virginia and Wisconsin. Anti-Gay Marriage Measures, *supra* note 27.

35. National Gay and Lesbian Task Force, Issue Map: Relationship Recognition for Same-Sex Couples in the U.S. (Feb. 22, 2008), http://thetaskforce.org/downloads/reports/issue_maps/relation-ship_recognition_2_08_color.pdf (last visited Apr. 21, 2008).

36. See Bowers v. Hardwick, 478 U.S. 186 (1986), overruled by Lawrence v. Texas, 539 U.S. 558(2003).

37. See 10 U.S.C. §654 (1993).

38. Servicemembers Legal Defense Network, Fact Sheet: Total "Don't Ask, Don't Tell" Discharges1994–2006, http://www.sldn.org/binary-data/SLDN_ARTICLES/pdf_file/3864.pdf (last visited Jan.24, 2008).

39. See Stephen Benjamin, *Don't Ask, Don't Translate*, N.Y. TIMES, June 8, 2007, at A29.

40. Australia, Austria, Belgium, Britain, Canada, Czech Republic, Denmark, Estonia, Finland, France, Germany, Ireland, Italy, Lithuania, Luxembourg, Netherlands, New Zealand, Norway, Slovenia, Spain, Sweden and Switzerland allow lesbians and gay men to serve. Servicemembers Legal Defense Network, Fact Sheet: Foreign

Militaries Which Allow Open Service, http://www.sldn.org/templates/dadt/record .html?section=145&record=1904 (last visited Jan. 24, 2008).

41. In *Lustig-Prean v. United Kingdom*, the European Court of Human Rights reviewed the British laws: By virtue of section 1(1) of the Sexual Offences Act 1967, homosexual acts in private between two consenting adults (at the time meaning 21 years or over) ceased to be criminal offences. However, such acts continued to constitute offences under the Army and Air Force Acts 1955and the Naval Discipline Act 1957 (Section 1(5) of the 1967 Act). Section 1(5) of the 1967Act was repealed by the Criminal Justice and Public Order Act 1994 (which Act also reduced the age of consent to 18 years). However, section 146(4) of the 1994 Act provided that nothing in that section prevented a homosexual act (with or without other acts or circumstances) from constituting a ground for discharging a member of the armed forces. Lustig-Prean v. United Kingdom, 29 Eur. Ct. H.R. 548, ¶ 37 (1999).

42. *Id.* ¶ 105.

43. See AARON BELKIN, *Don't Ask, Don't Tell: Is the Gay Ban Based on Military Necessity?*, 33 PARAMETERS 108, 110 (2003), available at http://www.carlisle.army .mil/usawc/Parameters/03summer/belkin.pdf.

Periodical and Internet Sources Bibliography

The following articles have been chosen to supplement the diverse views presented in this chapter.

Andrea Birdsall	"The 'Monster That We Need to Slay?' Global Governance, the United States, and the International Criminal Court," *Global Governance*, October–December 2010.
Mason C. Clutter	"Guantanamo Ten Years after 9/11," *Human Rights*, Winter 2011.
Amitai Etzioni	"Obama's Implicit Human Rights Doctrine," *Human Rights Review*, March 2011.
Tom Farer	"Un-Just War Against Terrorism and the Struggle to Appropriate Human Rights," *Human Rights Quarterly*, May 2008.
William A. Fletcher	"International Human Rights and the Role of the United States," *Northwestern University Law Review*, Winter 2010.
James Kirschick	"When a Nod's Not Enough," *Advocate*, February 10, 2009.
Harold Hongju Koh	"Restoring America's Human Rights Reputation," *Cornell International Law Journal*, Fall 2007.
Tod Lindberg	"A Way Forward with the International Criminal Court," *Policy Review*, February–March 2010.
Andrew C. McCarthy	"Enter Totalitarian Democracy," *New Criterion*, April 2012.
Amitabh Pal	"Blanket Immunity," *Progressive*, January 2007.

**OPPOSING
VIEWPOINTS®
SERIES**

CHAPTER 3

What Is the Impact of Religion on Human Rights?

Chapter Preface

Throughout Europe, numerous countries have discussed and in some cases legislated bans on Islamic clothing, prayer in schools, and the building of new Islamic architecture. While the controversy has been highlighted most recently in countries where Muslims make up a minority of the population, such as France and Germany, even in Turkey, a country that is predominantly Muslim, religious bans have existed for decades. These secular laws have sparked considerable debate regarding the human right to practice one's religion freely without impedance from the government.

The non-governmental human rights organization, Human Rights Watch (HRW), has spoken against the action taken by European governments to limit public expressions of Islam in schools and the civil service. The organization maintains that these bans violate international human rights standards. In the introduction to the organization's February 2009 report, "Discrimination in the Name of Neutrality: Headscarf Bans for Teachers and Civil Servants in Germany," Haleh Chahrokh, an HRW researcher, says, "These laws in Germany clearly target the headscarf, forcing women who wear it to choose between their jobs and their religious beliefs. . . . They discriminate on the grounds of both gender and religion and violate these women's human rights." HRW further equates bans on wearing religious clothing with other nations' laws forcing women to wear religious garments, arguing that both situations deprive women of their ability to act autonomously, protect their privacy, and freely express themselves.

In the face of this opposition, many proponents of the bans have defended the need to enforce such legislation. As politicians and citizens in France debated whether to institute a ban on headscarves a February 1, 2004, *Time* magazine article presented pro and con views of the legislation. In arguing for the ban, Therese Duplaix, the principal of a French secondary school, maintains, "A French state school is supposed to be a place of liberty where critical reason can be exercised. . . . Secularism allows us to build on the attributes that unite us, and not those that separate us." She views the bans as a means by which to combat intimidation and coercion based on religious principles. So far, the Court of Human Rights has ruled in favor of those who share Duplaix's view. In separate cases in both 2004 and 2008, involving the Turkish and French bans respectively, the court found that headscarf bans in public schools did not constitute a violation of human rights. According to German broadcaster Deutsche Welle, a press release from the court reported, "It was clear that the applicants' religious convictions were fully taken into account in relation to the requirements of protecting the rights and freedoms of others and public order."

The headscarf ban is only one circumstance in which religion and human rights intersect in today's global society. In the following chapter, authors explore whether religion infringes upon human rights or if religious freedom is being eroded.

> *"Challenged in many developing*
> *nations, religious freedom is also a*
> *human rights stepchild in the West."*

Religious Freedom as a Human Right Is Being Threatened Worldwide

Eric Schulzke

The author of the following viewpoint highlights the discrimination and violence leveled against minority religious groups in Southeast Asia and the Middle East. He points out that in some countries the government has institutionalized the bias, either officially or through a lack of action to combat it. Further, he contends that while these conditions may not be entirely surprising in certain contexts, religious freedom as a human right has been relegated to a secondary right even in the West. Eric Schulzke is a policy and politics writer for the Deseret News *newspaper who received his doctorate in political science from the University of California, Berkeley.*

As you read, consider the following questions:

1. According to the author, how has impunity empowered those who discriminate against religious minorities?

2. How many countries abstained from participating in the 1948 Universal Declaration of Human Rights vote, as stated by the author?
3. How do human rights activists in the United States treat freedom of religion, as described by Schulzke?

The images are so ghastly that Al Jazeera froze the video, allowing only voices to tell the tale. An Indonesian mob shouting "Allah Akbar" ["God Is Great"] surrounded three men at the doorway of their mosque, stripped them naked and beat them to death with stones, sticks and machetes. Police officers stood by, helpless or indifferent.

The victims of the February 2011 killings were members of Ahmadiyya, a tiny Muslim sect considered blasphemers by many Muslims because they believe their 19th-century founder was a prophet. In strict Islamic tradition, blasphemy is punishable by death.

Indonesia is a single wave in a rising tide of religious intolerance worldwide. Trouble spots span the globe, with hundreds of incidents in scores of countries each year. In some, the suppression of religious freedom is dehumanizing but not life-threatening; in others, the risk of genocide or "religious cleansing" is real, immediate and growing.

In response, the United States has tried to appeal to universal values and international agreements as it seeks to shame, badger or entice problem nations to reform. But the universality of those values has frayed in recent years, and the elite consensus at home to shore them up is shaky.

Inaction Increases Intolerance

Indonesia is justly viewed as a hopeful model of Islamic tolerance and democracy. But in 2005 the Indonesian Ulama Council [the country's highest Muslim clerical body] issued a decree declaring the Ahmadiyya "outside Islam" and "deviant" and urged the government to bar Ahmadis from proselytizing or public worship. Two key government officials soon signed a decree ordering the Ahmadiyya to stop teachings that "deviate from the principal teachings of Islam" and to stop teaching "that there is another prophet with his own teachings after Prophet Mohammed." Against the tide, Indonesia's largest Islamic organization opposed these moves, arguing that it "violates freedom of religion which is guaranteed by the constitution."

In July 2010, large mobs repeatedly tried to vandalize an Ahmadiyya mosque in West Java, while local police made minimal efforts to control the crowd. "When the Indonesian authorities sacrifice the rights of religious minorities to appease hardline Islamist groups, this simply causes more violence," said Elaine Pearson of Human Rights Watch in a press release. "While the police rightly stopped mobs from entering the mosque, their failure to arrest a single person will only embolden these groups to use violence again."

The subsequent killings proved Pearson right. Within weeks of that event, extremists sent four book bombs to Indonesian public figures. All were prominent voices for tolerance. There were no fatalities, but the message was clear.

Discrimination and Impunity Have Proliferated Worldwide

Indonesia's failure to make arrests in the mosque riot is known in human rights circles as "impunity"—the gap where a state lets perpetrators walk and cannot protect their victims. Impunity is a vicious circle, experts say, as violence escalates.

The springboard of impunity is often official discrimination. In Pakistan, four million Ahmadiyya are literally treated as noncitizens. To get a passport, Pakistanis must sign an oath that they consider the Ahmadi founder an "impostor prophet" and his followers "non-Muslims." Being a marked heretic can be tantamount to a death sentence. Pakistan's 2.8 million Christians are also at risk, and in March 2011 Shahbaz Bhatti, the Christian minister of minority affairs, was assassinated after he opposed blasphemy laws. The killer was never arrested.

Both official discrimination and impunity are common in religious persecution hotspots. In Nigeria, violence is edging toward civil war, as northern Muslims engage in unchecked retribution cycles with southern Christians. In Iraq, half of an ancient Christian population has fled, while others seek refuge in the Kurdish north. In Iran and Afghanistan, converts to Christianity face execution. In Egypt, Christian Copts are under siege, and 24 were murdered and hundreds were injured by Egyptian security forces in October 2011.

"We have found that an increase in government restrictions on religion coincides with a spike in religious persecution and violence," said Brian Grim at the Pew Research Center. Impunity seeps into the social fabric, experts say.

"In Pakistan, there have been numerous cases where neighbors get into a fight, and to settle scores one will invoke blasphemy laws," said Leonard Leo, the chairman of the U.S. Commission on International Religious Freedom. "When you abuse a minority you create an unstable and insecure environment for everyone."

Leo points to Nigeria, where he says the Islamist group Boka Haram—which means "Western education is sacrilege"—targets Christians in the south, but in their northern home the group has killed far more Muslims than Christians.

Religious Freedom Is Not Accepted as a Universal Human Right

Despite their failings, all these countries claim to accept the 1948 Universal Declaration of Human Rights, which holds that everyone "has the right to freedom of thought, conscience and religion" including the right "to change his religion or belief" and to "manifest his religion or belief in teaching, practice, worship and observance."

The universality of the Universal Declaration of Human Rights is central to its force. "The modern idea of religious tolerance grew not out of the West," said John Shattuck in a 2002 Harvard address, "but out of a universal revulsion after World War II towards genocide and crimes against humanity." An assistant secretary of state for human rights under President Bill Clinton, Shattuck glossed over the European Enlightenment— itself a product of horrific religious wars—and the American Founding that sprung from it.

But Shattuck's effort to universalize tolerance hides a shaky foundation. In fact, the religion clause of human rights declaration is quite challenging for many authoritarian and Islamic governments. Apostasy from Islam and blasphemy against it are widely seen as capital crimes, and non-Muslims have historically faced discrimination (dhimmi status) in exchange for a modicum of tolerance. Authoritarian governments, meanwhile, view uncontrolled religious passions as threats to public order.

It was thus no surprise that the eight abstentions from the 1948 declaration vote were seven Soviet bloc countries— and Saudi Arabia. The tension within Islam escalated in 1990, when the 45 member states of the Organization of the Islamic Conference meeting in Cairo signed an alternative Declaration of Human Rights in Islam. The Cairo declaration offers neither religious freedom nor any of the other vital rights outlined in 1948. It has been roundly criticized, but it signals the height of the hurdles.

Religious Freedom Is Downplayed in the West

Challenged in many developing nations, religious freedom is also a human rights stepchild in the West. For example, one of the most prominent advocacy groups is Human Rights Watch, which has taken religious persecution very seriously in individual cases. And yet while Human Rights Watch has special program officers in several areas—arms, health and human rights; children's rights; women's rights; and lesbian, gay, bisexual and

Social Hostilities Toward and Government Restrictions on Religion, 2009

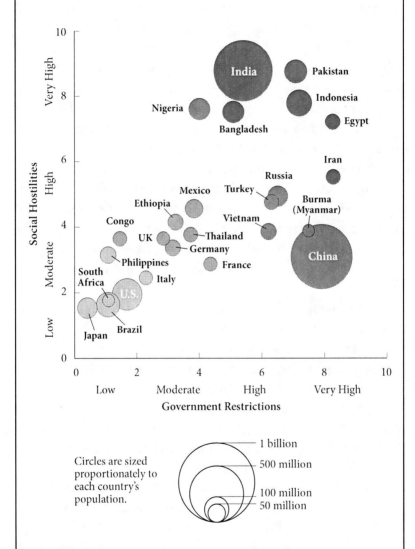

Circles are sized proportionately to each country's population.

1 billion
500 million
100 million
50 million

Note: Only the twenty-five most populous countries are presented in this graph.

TAKEN FROM: Pew Forum on Religion and Public Life, "Rising Restrictions on Religion," August 9, 2011, www.pewforum.org.

transgender rights—it has no such program for minority religions or religious freedom.

"While there are many in the human rights community, at the State Department, and at U.S. embassies who do excellent work to combat religious persecution, historically, there have been many others in these realms who, in practice, have treated religious freedom as inferior to certain other core human rights," said John Hanford who served as U.S. Ambassador at Large for International Religious Freedom from 2002 to 2009. "This was particularly true prior to the passage of the International Religious Freedom Act of 1998," he added.

In 1998, many diplomatic and advocacy elites opposed congressional action to entrench religious freedom in U.S. policy as a core human right. Secretary of State Madeleine Albright said doing so would create a "hierarchy of human rights," and some objected to the key role of evangelicals and Catholics in supporting the agenda, fearing these were out to advance Christianity abroad.

In his Harvard address noted above, Shattuck called out what he described as "threats to religious tolerance" at home, accusing the Religious Right of seeking to "promote special religious interests overseas." The vehicle for this, he said, was the International Religious Freedom Act of 1998.

"The burden is probably on the U.S. government to show that in this Act they're not engaging in, crusading or proselytization on behalf of the Christian religion," said Jemera Rone of Human Rights Watch at a 1999 conference in Hartford, Conn.

Shattuck further expanded his critique in a 2007 Pew forum, arguing that the International Religious Freedom Act is a stalking horse for missionary work. Pushing the freedom to openly live one's religion and to change religions could undermine social balance among people that "may or may not want to change their faith," Shattuck argued. The goal of tolerance should be to reduce religious conflict, not to expand religious freedom, he said. There is danger in taking universal human rights too literally, Shattuck suggested, and religious freedom practiced too robustly can be provocative.

The view of these skeptics was that "religious persecution should be vigorously opposed," wrote Thomas Farr of the Berkeley Center for Religion, Peace and World Affairs in a recent book. "But religion itself was not seen as a human good to be nourished. Rather, it is more often a source of conflict to be managed via tolerance."

Freedom of Religion Clashes with Secular Human Rights

Some human rights advocates also feared that emphasizing religion would undermine their agenda for less traditional and more secular human rights. The tension reaches back to the 1994 United Nations population control conference in Cairo, where the Clinton administration and its allies hoped for major breakthroughs on abortion, family planning, the redefinition of marriage and children's rights. To the administration's surprise, a powerful counter movement developed, led by a religious coalition of Catholics, other Christians and Muslims. In the end, all the controversial proposals were defeated in a fractious conference. When the congressional religious freedom agenda was launched three years later, the last thing secularist rights advocates wanted was to share the field with such contrarians.

Jeffrey Goldberg highlighted the tension in a 1997 *New York Times* article. He noted an odd conversation between religious freedom agitator Michael Horowitz and Kenneth Roth, the director of Human Rights Watch. Horowitz was building a coalition of religious leaders for religious freedom and wanted Roth to meet with the Christian Coalition about religious freedom abroad. Roth immediately questioned the group's position on abortion, and Horowitz was stunned at the non sequitur. Roth said he told Horowitz that certain evangelical views "are contrary to the views of the human rights movement, around the issue of the rights of women, and around the issue of religious tolerance, but we are here to defend the rights of all, including the intolerant."

In short, the same voices that suspected Western religious imperialism in the religious freedom movement were firmly committed to spreading their own secular version of universal Western values. As Thomas Farr wrote, the new religious freedom activists "represented a traditionalist version of Christianity that would very likely contest the administration's vision of human rights. If this kind of religious advocacy got a foothold in the foreign policy establishment, it could mean trouble."

"[The ban on defamation of religions] is turning out to be a cover-up for the murderous instigators of religious tension and reactionary self-censorship."

Freedom of Religion Threatens Freedom of Speech

Miklos Haraszti

In the following viewpoint, a journalist and scholar identifies defamation of religion bans as one of the greatest threats to freedom of speech today. He argues that under the guise of diplomacy, these bans have actually promoted censorship and supported oppressive government regimes that seek to limit free speech to remain in control. The author maintains the bans not only diminish freedom of speech but also provoke the violence they intend to decrease. Miklos Haraszti is a Hungarian writer, international and public affairs professor at Columbia Law School, and advocate of human rights.

As you read, consider the following questions:

1. As stated by the author, how was the vote on the defamation of religion ban broken down?

Miklos Haraszti, "In God's Name: The Growing Trend of Criminalising Criticism of Religion Is a Declaration of War on Freedom of Speech," *Index on Censorship*, vol. 38, no. 2, 2009. Copyright © 2009 by Index on Censorship. All rights reserved. Reproduced by permission.

2. How have journalists been punished for disobeying the defamation of religion ban, according to Haraszti?
3. What is the "extremism package" of laws that has emerged from the defamation ban, as defined by the author?

It should no longer be difficult to tackle illegitimate limits to free speech, particularly since so many dictatorships have now made the transition to democracy. The required standards are clear enough: actual instigations to actual crimes must be seen as crimes, but otherwise offensive speech should be handled by encouraging further dialogue—in the press, through media ethics bodies or in civil courts.

What we see instead, despite some progress internationally in decriminalising violations of honour and dignity, is a growing, punitive trend that is introducing new speech bans into national criminal codes.

One of these à la mode speech crimes is defamation of history—committed in some countries by questioning a nation's historical narrative and in others by defending it. While Turkey prosecutes writers for using the word genocide to describe the massacre of Armenians in 1915, Switzerland has prosecuted a Turkish politician for calling the use of the term genocide an "international lie". Yet defamation of religions is proving to be an even more insidious and restrictive pattern worldwide.

A Declaration of War on Freedom of Expression

On 26 March [2009], the UN [United Nations] Human Rights Council passed a resolution condemning "defamation of religions" as a human rights violation, despite wide concerns that it could be used to justify curbs on free speech. The Council adopted the non-binding text, proposed by Pakistan on behalf of the Islamic states, with a vote of 23 states in favour and 11 against, with 13 abstentions. The resolution "Combating Defamation of

Religions" has been passed, revised and passed again every year since 1999, except in 2006, in the UN Human Rights Council (HRC) and its predecessor, the UN Human Rights Commission. It is promoted by the persistent sponsorship of the Organisation of the Islamic Conference with the acknowledged objective of getting it codified as a crime in as many countries as possible, or at least promoting it into a universal anathema. Alongside this campaign, there is a global undercurrent of violence and ready-made self-censorship that has surrounded all secular and artistic depictions of Islamic subjects since the [Salman] Rushdie fatwa [which called for the author's execution after the publication of his book *The Satanic Verses*, which portrayed the prophet Mohammed negatively in the eyes of some Muslim leaders].

This year's resolution, unlike previous versions, no longer ignores Article 19, the right to free expression. That crucial human right has now received a mention, albeit in a context which misleadingly equates defamation of religions with incitement to hatred and violence against religious people, and on that basis denies it the protection of free speech. It also attempts to bracket criticism of religion with racism.

On the other hand, the vague parameters of possible defamation cases have now grown to include the "targeting" of symbols and venerated leaders of religion by the media and the Internet. What we are witnessing may be an effort at diplomacy, but it is also a declaration of war on twenty-first century media freedoms by a coalition of latter-day authoritarians.

The Defamation Clause Supports Oppressive Governments

There is nothing backward looking or historicising in the declaration. It adopts the language of human rights so that the proposal sounds compatible with the advanced multiculturalism of liberal democracies. All the signatories have acquiesced: the late-communist and the post-communist governments among them, along with the post-colonial or predominantly Muslim nations. Yet only very few of the 23, amongst them South Africa and Indonesia, are democracies equipped with a truly pluralistic media. The consistently high number of abstentions, including by nations with free speech guarantees, helps ensure the proposition is officially accepted every year.

Because of this contemporary strategy, I reject the often heard claim that the resolution's backers represent a culturally defined movement. That claim would only serve to offer another excuse to patronise the endeavour, and leniently underestimate its impact. In fact, the drive to criminalise defamation of religions is an entirely post-modern, Orwellian [after author George Orwell, meaning totalitarian or oppressive] spin crusade against human dignity, ostensibly in its name.

Year after year, the Human Rights Council (HRC) vote lends a double domestic victory to the support [of] oppressive governments. It cements their control of speech through cultural taboos and blasphemy laws, and at the same time glorifies and internationally acknowledges them in the vanguard of promoting tolerance.

The Inaction of Moderates Opens the Door for Extremists

Of course, one can understand why many democracies condescendingly abstain from the fight and let the game of the Organisation of the Islamic Conference prevail. After all, since the Iranian Revolution and the global debut of al Qaeda, those willing to present the oppressive notion of defamation of religions in human rights terms are by definition moderates, compared to the jihadists who openly reject those rights. The HRC manoeuvres also help the moderates to counter claims by domestic radicals that their governments are not true guardians of the faith.

I happen to remember these games from my time in the closed civilisation of the communist one-party state [of the Soviet Union], where pluralism consisted of factional fights inside the Politburo of the Party. Kremlinologists also knew the game, but they must have had more fun watching it than I had. The technique was called "overtaking from the left", and it meant the recurring scene whereby otherwise pragmatic leaders of the Party started to emanate hardliner slogans, obviously in order to keep the Stalinists at bay. It actually never simply meant just tough talk; it always came with new measures against freethinkers, such as house searches and indictments, "only" to provide proofs of the leadership's fidelity to the cause. This tactic is a distant relative of the "taking the wind out of the sails" policy of western moderate parties, when they buy into anti-immigration measures in order to preclude a growing popularity of xenophobic platforms that propose . . . anti-immigration measures.

Defamation Laws Lead to Punishment for Open Expression

The trouble is that "taking the wind out of the sails" may help one stay on board, but never succeeds in easing the restrictions. Let me tell you how it really works when the stipulations of the Human Rights Council resolution are applied.

In Azerbaijan—one of the supporters of the resolution—two journalists were given prison sentences in 2007. Rafiq Tagi, a journalist of the intellectual monthly *Senet*, and Samir Sadagatoglu, the newspaper's editor, were sentenced to three and four years respectively, for alleged "incitement to religious hatred" in a philosophical essay published in 2006. In fact, the essay compared European and Islamic values in a somewhat self-critical vein. (The language was "them and us".) Its thesis was innocent, well-meaning and polite. It was a similar message about a similar subject, "reason and faith", to Pope Benedict XVI's famous Regensburg speech the same year. In my assessment, it was even milder, as there were no Byzantine quotations ascribing violent proselytism to Mohammed. The question of violence did not even turn up in the text.

Previously, an Iranian grand ayatollah, Fazel Lankarani, had issued a fatwa calling for the two journalists to be killed. Domestic religious activists responded by starting an intimidation campaign against the journalists. Reportedly, they were allowed to shout death threats in the courtroom. The journalists' crime was defamation of religion (their own, apparently) and incitement, by the same act, to religious hatred (against themselves, one must conclude). Yet it was the journalists who sat in the dock, not those who menaced them with violence.

And, most importantly, the Iranian ayatollah who called for their death was never accused of incitement, neither in Azerbaijan nor in Iran—protected as he was by his status as a defender, rather than a defamer, of the faith.

Newspapers Are Closed for Defamation of Religion

Similar abuses could be cited from several non-Muslim countries as well, all of them, by the way, participating states of the OSCE [Organization for Security and Co-operation in Europe], and some of them members of the Council of Europe. The commitments of the former and the standards of the latter would forbid any persecution based on "defamation of religions". But under the justifying umbrella of the HRC resolutions (and exploiting the lack of resolute opposition to them in Europe) the crisis created around the Danish cartoons [of Mohammed] was used to get tough on critically minded outlets and journalists.

In Russia, the Vologda newspaper *Nash Region* published a collage of the cartoons on 15 February 2006, as part of an article on the global controversy. The proprietor decided to close the newspaper shortly afterwards in order to ease the legal consequences. Prosecutors had immediately opened a case against the editor, Anna Smirnova, for "inciting religious hatred". In April 2006, she was fined 100,000 roubles (approximately US $3,000) and given a two-year suspended sentence. Happily, a month later, the Vologda Oblast Court overturned the decision on ap-

Discussion of Religion Will Sometimes Shock and Offend

The legal theory of "Defamation of Religions" is a vague, over-broad principle designed to provide protection specifically for Islam and to allow Islamic nations to impermissibly limit the expressions of others within their countries. The U.N. [United Nations] should not continue to adopt the resolutions on defamation of religions as they encourage overbroad statutes giving governments the power to arbitrarily decide what constitutes defamation and should therefore be regulated or even criminalized. The negative effects of such broad-reaching statues have already been demonstrated in multiple countries.

Rather than encourage the promulgation of defamation of religions legislation, the U.N. must use established international law principles and guidelines of incitement to discrimination and violence to encourage States to enforce religious rights, limit discrimination, and create an atmosphere of mutual respect through a suitably narrow notion of incitement that will allow some regulation and even criminalization, but that will continue to allow robust discussion that sometimes shocks and offends.

Allison G. Belnap, "Defamation of Religions: A Vague and Overbroad Theory that Threatens Basic Human Rights," Brigham Young University Law Review, *January 1, 2010.*

peal. It was clear no happy ending would have been possible had the paper still existed.

Exactly the same scenario was played out in Volgograd: the publisher of *Gorodskie Vesti* decided to close the newspaper after charges for defamation and incitement were brought by the regional branch of the country's ruling party, United Russia. Criminal proceedings were subsequently dropped. The trigger for the prosecution was a sweet, truly peace-preaching caricature of the four venerated personalities Moses, Jesus, Mohammed and Buddha. In the cartoon, the religious leaders are watching television and concerned to see demonstrators from different religions hurling insults at each other. "This is not what we have taught you to do", one of the prophets is saying.

In Belarus, Alexander Zdvizhkov, editor of the *Zhoda* opposition newspaper, was sentenced to three years in prison on 18 January 2008 for incitement of religious hatred. His newspaper was shut down in March 2006 for merely planning to publish the cartoons, and remains closed today. Zdvizhkov went into hiding abroad, was then arrested upon return, and finally released after the Supreme Court reduced his sentence from three years to three months, the term he had already served.

Bans Now Include Defamation of Government

But these were only opportunistic blitzes. Since the cartoons crisis, another new punitive fashion has emerged, also inspired by the HRC resolutions: the extremism package. In Russia (which came up with the idea), Belarus, Kazakhstan, Kyrgyzstan, Moldova and Tajikistan, legislators have bundled the defamation of religions provisions with otherwise legitimate incitement laws, adding also the ban of "offensive criticism" (yes, defamation) of government bodies or officials. This cocktail of legislation is presented as a heightened form of combating a never precisely defined attitude—extremism. There is an echo here of the West's promotion of terrorism provisions, which is helpful in defusing possible criticism. But while western legislation was criticised domestically as being *possibly* conducive to illegitimate prosecution of political thought, the eastern extremism packages are *actually* created for that purpose. And they are used, too, especially in retaliation for unwanted coverage of the human rights situation in the Northern Caucasus.

At the time of writing, Slovakia is planning to introduce its own "extremism" package, ostensibly to fight radicalism. Ireland—while otherwise decriminalising libel—is about to introduce a new crime, "blasphemous libel", described as an act of compliance with a constitutional tenet dating from the 1930s. Is it far-fetched to see here an implicit, perhaps even unconscious, influence of the HRC campaign? When I referred earlier to the surrounding threat of violence, I meant the disturbing, but untold, connection between the recurring legal drive at the UN Human Rights Council and the fatwas, murders and violent demonstrations against secular or critical depictions of Islamic issues. The grievances expressed by the fatwa authors and the HRC diplomats are in fact indistinguishable. What is missing here is the realisation that combating defamation of religions is not just harmful: it is the wrong fight, the wrong criminalisation.

I do not see any moral difference between ordering a contracted killing of investigative reporters like Anna Politkovskaya and issuing fatwas that call for murdering writers or journalists. Both punish writers for doing their job. And, by the way, the fatwas also offer financial rewards, just like the *zakazchiki* in Russia.

Violence Has Been Sanctioned

In Pakistan, the main country sponsor of this year's HRC resolution, Mohammed Yousaf Qureshi, prayer leader at the historic Mohabat Khan mosque in Peshawar, announced in 2006 that the mosque and his religious school would give US $25,000 and a car, while a local jewellers association offered another US $1m, for the murder of any Danish cartoonist. In India, Uttar Pradesh Minister for Haj and Minority Welfare Haji Yaqoob Qureshi placed a 510m Indian rupee (US $11m) bounty on the head of a cartoonist, plus the murderer's weight in gold. I am listing here examples only from inside democracies that signed the HRC resolutions or abstained.

At this point, the resolution is no longer an exercise at taking the wind out of the sails of the radicals. It is turning out to be a cover-up for the murderous instigators of religious tension and reactionary self-censorship.

I find it a scandal that authors of edicts calling for the murder of writers or journalists can still continue to be respected and do not have to face the consequences of their hateful acts, while many journalists have to live anonymously under police protection. So far, none of the names of the instigators of these fatwas has appeared on wanted lists, not even in the countries which, I am sure, would extradite the masterminds of Politkovskaya's murder, if found. That is the HRC resolution's longest shadow.

Caution is somewhat understandable in a country such as tiny Denmark, stricken by calls for a commercial boycott, or in any single nation. But what about the European Union? Has it not been designed to be stronger than its components? What about Interpol and other international law enforcement agencies? Since when have they dropped soliciting murder from their list of crimes? What about at least a travel ban against the well-known *zakazchiki* of religious hate crimes?

The Human Rights Council must be told: if incitement to religious hatred is what you are concerned about, call immediately for the punishment of those who issue fatwas inciting violence. There can be no stronger protection against defamation of Islam or any faith. Promote tolerance by relieving the fear factor from the minds of the world's editors.

> *"'Islamic' states—like 'Islamic rights'—*
> *fail to respect the basic necessities of*
> *conscience and expression and tend to*
> *suppress dissent."*

Islam Is Incompatible with Human Rights

Austin Dacey and Colin Koproske

The authors of the following viewpoint trace the history of the Islamic human rights movement and its incompatibility with the larger human rights movement, as based on the United Nations' Universal Declaration of Human Rights. The authors argue that Islamic human rights documents in fact limit human rights by relying on Islamic exceptionalism and demanding that all rights comply with Shari'ah law. Austin Dacey is an author and human rights activist who serves as a representative to the United Nations for the International Humanist and Ethical Union; Colin Koproske is completing his graduate study at Oxford University and is the founder of the University of Southern California Secular Alliance.

As you read, consider the following questions:

1. As stated by the authors, how do the English and Arabic versions of the Universal Islamic Declaration of Human Rights differ?

Austin Dacey and Colin Koproske, "Islam and Human Rights: Defending Universality and the United Nations," *Free Inquiry*, vol. 29, no. 1, December 2008–January 2009. Copyright © 2009 by the Center for Inquiry. All rights reserved. Reproduced by permission.

2. What does the Cairo Declaration say about free speech, according to Dacey and Koproske?

3. What do the authors fear will result from the ongoing movement towards acceptance of Islamic rights?

Sixty years have passed since the issuance of the world's first and greatest statement in favor of universal human rights, the Universal Declaration of Human Rights (UDHR). Today both the document and the institution put in place to protect its ideals (what has, since 2006, been called the U.N. [United Nations] Human Rights Council) are threatened more than ever. There is now an alternative human rights system, infused with religious language and layered with exceptions, omissions, and caveats. The movement toward "Islamic human rights" (IHR) has been successfully presented to the Human Rights Council (HRC) as merely "complementary" to the UDHR. The meager opposition to this subversion is suppressed, as "religious matters" are increasingly forbidden from discussion in U.N. chambers. Western powers have either failed to stand up for the UDHR or have withdrawn from the human rights discussion altogether. In what follows, we will trace the development of these worrying trends.

Islamic Exceptionalism in Human Rights Observance

The Universal Islamic Declaration of Human Rights (UIDHR) provides a useful starting point. While opposition to the UDHR under the banner of conservative Islam was widespread even at its inception in 1948, this 1981 document was the first official political statement of Islamic exceptionalism in the realm of human rights. The UIDHR was written by representatives from Egypt, Pakistan, Saudi Arabia, and various other Muslim states under the auspices of the London-based Islamic Council, a private organization affiliated with the conservative Muslim World League. It drew little criticism as it was rife with ambiguous, equivocal language and had an English translation that masked many of its overt religious references. In its original Arabic, the UIDHR often requires Islamic considerations that limit rather than enshrine human rights as outlined by international norms. For example, compare the English and Arabic versions of Article 12, which outlines the "Right to Freedom of Belief, Thought and Speech":

English: "Every person has the right to express his thoughts and beliefs so long as he remains within the limits prescribed by the Law. No one, however, is entitled to disseminate falsehood or to circulate reports that may outrage public decency, or to indulge in slander, innuendo, or to cast defamatory aspersions on other persons."

Arabic: "Everyone may think, believe and express his ideas and beliefs without interference or opposition from anyone as long as he obeys the limits [hudud] set by the shari'ah [Islamic law]. It is not permitted to spread falsehood [al-batil] or disseminate that which involves encouraging abomination [al-fahisha] or forsaking the Islamic community [takhdhil li'l-umma]."

The English version reads as an innocuous restatement of well-established norms, embracing rights to speech and generally accepted limits involving slander and libel. In its original Arabic, however, this article demonstrates a clear religious test for speech: one may not express oneself beyond the limits set by Islamic law, and one must not "encourage abomination" or "forsake" the Islamic community. The concepts of "falsehood," "encouraging abomination," and "forsaking" are unclear and dangerously open to potential abuse by religious courts. It is apparent that it is not citizens who are protected, but the *umma* (Muslim community). The rubric of judgment is not public law, not universal standards of justice, but *shari'ah* (Islamic law).

In 1984, Iran's U.N. representative, Said Raja'l Khorasani, said the following amid allegations of human rights violations:

[Iran] recognized no authority . . . apart from Islamic law . . . conventions, declarations and resolutions or decisions of international organizations, which were contrary to Islam, had no validity in the Islamic Republic of Iran. . . . The Universal Declaration of Human Rights, which represented secular understanding of the Judaeo-Christian tradition, could not be implemented by Muslims and did not accord with the system of values recognized by the Islamic Republic of Iran; [t]his country would therefore not hesitate to violate its provisions.

In the complete version of this document, we critique the argument, expressed by Khorasani, that human rights do not apply beyond the borders of Judeo-Christian societies. At this point, it suffices to say that by the mid-1980s, a strong current of Islamic exceptionalism had established staunch opposition to the UDHR and the U.N. human rights agenda.

Islam, Not Human Rights, Are Protected

The Organization of the Islamic Conference (OIC), created in 1969, would take up the mantle of Islamic solidarity established by the Islamic Council and Muslim World League; it is now the preeminent Islamic institution, with fifty-seven member states and a powerful presence in global politics. Even with such a large membership, the OIC has a clear political posture; tasked with "liberating Jerusalem and Al-Aqsa from Zionist occupa-tion," strengthening "Islamic solidarity among Member States," coordinating action to "safeguard the Holy Places," and support-ing "the struggle of all Muslim people to safeguard their dignity, independence and national rights," this organization is built for conflict with the non-Muslim world.

The OIC's most significant entrance onto the field of human rights came in 1990, with the adoption of the Cairo Declaration on Human Rights in Islam. This document, affirmed by all fifty-seven member states and considered canon to this day, used much of the language from the 1981 UIDHR, this time making it clear (even in English) that "All the rights and freedoms stipulated in this Declaration are subject to the Islamic shari'ah," and that "The Islamic shari'ah is the only source of reference for the explanation or clarification of any of the articles of this Declaration" (Articles 24 and 25). In place of religious freedom, its authors issue what is in effect a prohibition against conversion from Islam: "Islam is the religion of unspoiled nature. It is prohibited to exercise any form of compulsion on man or to exploit his poverty or ignorance in order to convert him to another religion or to atheism." Article 22, the Cairo Declaration's "free speech" provision, clearly suggests that it is Islam, not the individual, that deserves protection:

(a) Everyone shall have the right to express his opinion freely in such manner as would not be contrary to the principles of the shari'ah.

(b) Everyone shall have the right to advocate what is right, and propagate what is good, and warn against what is wrong and evil according to the norms of Islamic shari'ah.

(c) Information is a vital necessity to society. It may not be exploited or misused in such a way as may violate sanctities and the dignity of Prophets, undermine moral and ethical values or disintegrate, corrupt or harm society or weaken its faith.

Surprisingly, the Cairo Declaration has received little attention from the international community. One reason for this lack of coverage is the continued suppression of criticism by members of the OIC, in conjunction with the so-called nonaligned states and powerful allies in the cause of weakening the U.N.'s human rights apparatus: Russia, China, and Cuba. Every year since 1999, a member of the OIC has proposed a resolution in the Human Rights Council (formerly the Human Rights Commission) called "Combating the Defamation of Religions," which decries the outbreak of "Islamophobia" across the globe and calls for greater efforts to curb defamation, discrimination,

Muslims' Difficulty with Human Rights

What makes it so difficult for Muslims to recognize and to practise universal human rights? First of all, the Islamic world understands itself as the "khair umma" (Surah 3,110), that is, as the best society on earth. From this standpoint, there are great inner barriers to recognizing the cultural achievements of non-Muslims and to learning from them. But, this is necessary for the Islamic world with regard to the European-influenced tradition of human rights. Instead, all non-Muslim influenced civilizations are devalued as *djahiliyya*, that is, as "the age of ignorance without knowledge of the revelation of God to Muhammed". Cultural achievements such as the Declaration of Human Rights are therefore considered of less value compared to Islam.

Rolf Hille, "Human Rights and Islam:
Is the 'Clash of Civilizations' Already
Preprogrammed?," Evangelical Review
of Theology, October 2006.

or hate speech against Muslims or the Islamic faith. This resolution has passed each year with nearly unanimous support.

The Islamic Lobby Internationalizes Blasphemy

On June 16, 2008, the Islamic lobby showed its power when representatives from Egypt and Pakistan silenced David Littman, who was speaking for the World Union for Progressive Judaism, during a statement to the Human Rights Council about women's rights and *shari'ah* law. Within twenty-two seconds, Littman was interrupted by a point of order from the Egyptian representative —the first of sixteen such interruptions. The representative and his Pakistani ally insisted that "Islam will not be crucified in this Council" and argued that any discussion of Islamic *shari'ah* was irrelevant and inappropriate.

After a forty-minute break, the presiding Council president, Doru Romulus Costea of Romania, announced that "The Council is not prepared to discuss religious questions and we don't have to do so. Declarations must avoid judgments or evaluation about religion." Such a statement institutes nothing less than a blasphemy taboo in the Human Rights Council. Members and speakers are effectively prohibited from speaking about the issuance of *fatwas*, the stoning of women for adultery, or the execution of apostates as it relates to Islam.

A month later, at a U.S. congressional panel on religious freedom, former U.S. State Department human rights expert Susan Bunn Livingstone suggested that proponents of such limitations on criticism "are trying to internationalize the concept of blasphemy. . . . They are using this discourse of 'defamation' to carve out any attention we would bring to a country. Abstractions like states and ideologies are seen as more important than individuals. This is a moral failure." The silencing of Littman's criticism takes place against a background of broader cultural clashes. From death threats and assassinations to lawsuits and op-eds, aggressive defenders of Islam have sought retribution against those who would disparage its name.

The Human Rights Council Undermines Free Expression

What has the Human Rights Council done about this? On March 28, 2008, the Council actually undermined its own ability to protect free speech. An amendment to a resolution on freedom of expression (passed 27 to 15 with three abstentions) now requires the U.N. Special Rapporteur on Freedom of Expression to "report on instances in which the abuse of the right of freedom of expression constitutes an act of racial or religious discrimination." Instead of traveling the world in search of instances in which free speech is unjustly limited, the Rapporteur will now do just the opposite, in an effort to police "abusive" speech. The protector has become the oppressor. The Council failed to note that Muslims (and all citizens) are already protected against discrimination and defamatory speech by Article 19 of the International Covenant on Civil and Political Rights, and reasonable limits to free speech were already referred to in the preamble to the March 28 resolution. Further, concerns for freedom of religion are already reported by the Special Rapporteur for Freedom of Religion.

With such protections already in place, this amendment's only effect is the undermining of what little ability the HRC has to safeguard free expression around the world.

While the HRC has been preoccupied with the fight against "Islamophobia," OIC member states have avoided confrontation by touting the compatibility of the Cairo Declaration and the UDHR, explaining that it simply adapts the letter and intent of the UDHR to the unique cultural context of Islam. In 2002, Mary Robinson, the High Commissioner for Human Rights at the U.N., appeased Islamic states in a speech to the OIC in which she confirmed that "No one can deny that at its core Islam is entirely consonant with the principles of fundamental human rights, including human dignity, tolerance, solidarity and equality. . . . And no one can deny the acceptance of the universality of human rights by Islamic States."

Unfortunately, an effort to point out the differences between Islamic and universal human rights by Roy Brown of the International Humanist and Ethical Union (IHEU) was silenced by Islamic representatives in predictable fashion. Even as Islamic states continually tout the prominence and exceptional quality of Islam in their conceptions of human rights, they successfully sell their commitment to universality and muffle the cries of critics all over the world.

The United States, which has held only observer status in the HRC, quietly withdrew from the Council entirely on June 6, 2008. A State Department spokesman complained that the Council "has really turned into a forum that seems to be almost solely focused on bashing Israel" and announced that the United States would only engage with the Council on matters of national security or compelling national interest. While we share the administration's concern about the notable politicization of the HRC, its complete disengagement from the world's most influential human rights body is worrying.

Islamic Rights Are Different than Human Rights

Why is this activity in the HRC so important? The yearly resolutions "Combating the Defamation of Religion" and the wider movement toward a formal Islamic charter on both international law and human rights may have a wider impact than many expect. International covenants and agreements are intended to be introduced into the municipal law of the states that endorse them. The UDHR, for example, has been a positive force primarily by virtue of its influence on the human rights norms of countless states since its inception. The new norms governing the discussion and defamation of religion, as well as the unraveling of human rights universality, could very well have the same effect.

The debate between universal and culturally specific human rights schemes is not merely an intellectual hobby of academics and diplomats—it has real consequences in state government. Just as members of the OIC have pushed through legal loopholes in order to escape international human rights standards, many Islamic states (and the Western multiculturalists who support their cultural sovereignty) have used relativist rhetoric as a foundation for marrying religion and politics in the Islamic world. This concession to Islamist philosophy, we argue, is not a show of cultural respect or the most prudent first step on the bridge to modernity. Instead, explicitly "Islamic" states—like "Islamic rights"—fail to respect the basic necessities of conscience and expression and tend to suppress dissent. . . .

The universal human rights agreed to by all United Nations members need philosophical and political defense, and the tools established to maintain those rights (i.e., the Human Rights Council and related offices) need reexamination. . . .

The trend of enshrining special protection for Islam (or more accurately, protection for rulers of Islamic states and their particular interpretations of Islam) is now pervasive. Will those who value human rights and free expression gather the will to resist this trend?

> "Human rights . . . are all too often
> dismissed as 'Western' and therefore
> not only irrelevant to Muslims, but
> also dangerous because they carry with
> them an imperialistic agenda."

Many Muslims Mistakenly Believe Human Rights Are Incompatible with Islam

Asma T. Uddin

The author of the following viewpoint argues that many Muslims have misunderstood the relationship between Islam and human rights. As a result of the association between human rights and the West, the author claims that most Muslims see rights such as liberty, religious freedom, and freedom of speech as encouraging a complete lack of rules, morality, and respect for Islam. Still, she maintains that if Muslims can succeed at engaging in dialogue on these issues and effectively define their culture, the gap between Islam and human rights can be bridged. Asma T. Uddin is an international law attorney with the Becket Fund for Religious Liberty and the founder of altmuslimah.com, a social and political news website exploring gender issues within the Muslim community.

Asma T. Uddin, "Burden of Proof: Personal Liberty, Islamic Faith, and Public Morality," *Patheos*, August 16, 2010. www.patheos.com. Copyright © 2010 by Patheos. All rights reserved. Reproduced by permission.

As you read, consider the following questions:

1. As stated by the author, how do states use religion to their benefit?
2. What is the misconception Muslims have about religious freedom, according to the author?
3. What does the author identify as the main problems facing the Muslim community?

My legal and advocacy work both in the U.S. and abroad has given me the unique opportunity to view challenges faced by the Muslim community in multifarious socio-political settings. What is clear to me is that the challenges faced, and to be faced in the coming century, by the Muslim community require the utilization of the same individual and societal instruments under evaluation. These include the appropriate and permissible application of individual and communal freedoms, the freedom as an individual to study one's faith and offer new and relevant interpretations of such, and the freedom for a community as a whole to practice its faith in the public and private sphere. And so, I see major challenges faced by the Muslim community in the 21st century as coming from two arenas: 1) intra-community differences—such as disparate interpretations of gender roles, or differing theological and historical critical interpretations of the Quran; and 2) extra-community relations—such as variant understandings of how self (Muslim) versus other (non-Muslim) should interact and the responsibilities of each toward the other.

Much of my legal and advocacy work while at the Becket Fund for Religious Liberty, a non-profit, non-partisan law firm that protects the free expression of all faiths, has been in Muslim communities in the Muslim world, particularly in Egypt and Pakistan, where the central short and long-term challenge is a government that is authoritarian and/or corrupt. State control of religion, whether through monitoring of mosque sermons or prosecution of "deviant" interpretations—Shia, Koranist,

Ahmadi, or even Sunni—under national security pretexts, politicizes religion so that "Islam" ultimately becomes a tool to be manipulated by the state to best serve its interests. The realization of religious freedom, free speech, and other fundamental human rights is dependent on adequate checks on government power. With activists routinely imprisoned and harassed, the countercurrent to government restrictions is always struggling to gather momentum.

Misconceptions About Human Rights Permeate the Muslim World

There is also a deeper misunderstanding among those in power about the nature of human rights. Human rights as articulated in international instruments are all too often dismissed as "Western" and therefore not only irrelevant to Muslims, but also dangerous because they carry with them an imperialistic agenda. Moreover, religious freedom is interpreted as part of not just Westernization but also the Christianization of the Muslim world. Recently in Morocco, Christian expatriates have been deported out of fear that their religious expression is disruptive to the stability of the country and represents the agenda of foreign governments. Similar deportations have occurred with Shias, underscoring again the intra-Muslim element to religious freedom restrictions.

Even among individual Muslims, the vast majority of whom are freedom-loving, there are several ingrained misconceptions about human rights. Religious freedom is conflated with anarchy, particularly of the sexual sort—the misconception being that religious freedom is ultimately about freedom from religion, which for many Muslims is freedom from moral constraints and thus total freedom to succumb to hedonism.

Liberty is, as such, confused with libertinism, whereas in fact these two sorts of freedom are entirely distinct. The freedom to be a human being with rights, duties, and consequences for one's actions is different than freedom from constraints. Like authoritarian approaches to freedom—the over-application of rules so that individuals are unable to make their own decisions —libertine approaches infantilize people. Rules are needed to help shape and develop society, but if everything is regulated by the state, people can never learn to regulate themselves.

Religious freedom, rooted in human dignity, not only does not create anarchy but also in fact leads to *more* public order; societies thrive when people are allowed to freely and peacefully express their deepest held beliefs. External oppression of religious expression does not eliminate it but forces it underground, often causing it to mutate into violent, extremist forms.

In the realm of free speech and free religious expression, I have heard all too often that "rights are limited"—that is, that we cannot conceive of rights without also articulating correspondent responsibilities and limitations. While this is no doubt true, and fully accounted for in every international human rights instrument, there seems to be a tendency among the Muslims I meet with abroad that the limits are somehow more important than the right itself. The limit—whether in the form of blasphemy laws, apostasy laws, or anti-conversion and anti-proselytization laws—is vaguely and broadly defined, thus leaving it to the whims of the individual, or worse, the government to interpret it as best suits its own interests. While theoretically, limitations make sense, as applied, the limit swallows the right. The push for anti-defamation measures at the United Nations is a good example of an attempt to "protect" the integrity of Islam by placing a restriction on freedom of speech.

To some extent, these biases can be found among American Muslims as well, particularly those who insist on self-ghettoization, which in turn positions them against or in contrast to the American majority rather than comfortably integrated within it. Even among the relatively better integrated members of the community, the biggest challenge when it comes to religious freedom is the articulation of proper strategies to overcome Islamophobia. Too often, Muslims resort to advocating legal sanctions on, for example, hate speech, rather than trying to understand approaches that are in the community's strategic interests. The result is that Muslims continue to be leveled with accusations of being anti-free speech and anti-religious freedom.

Dialogue with the Muslim Community Has Often Failed

As a religious freedom attorney, especially one regularly involved in media, I am very aware of the need to address the issues facing the international and domestic Muslim community by helping Muslims understand both the international human rights framework and the American constitutional framework. There is a need to translate these frameworks into terms that make sense culturally and theologically for Muslims.

While barriers to understanding and implementing human rights are the biggest challenge facing the community from within, particularly in the international context, from without, Islamophobia is a huge problem. The Danish cartoon controversy is a prominent case in which there was a marked failure of communication. An undoubtedly offensive portrayal of the Prophet led to an international fiasco as the Muslim community struggled to express the hurt and offense the cartoons had caused. However, language failed, and a segment of the international Muslim community turned to violence to express its anger.

The Muslim community often fails to successfully articulate to a non-Muslim audience its understanding of common norms. For example, it remains alienated largely on questions related to gender, whether it be veiling, women's rights, gender roles, and so on. At the same time, the community struggles within when it comes to realizing true gender equality. With forums such as my web magazine, Altmuslimah.com, it is possible to strive to fill that communication gap by fostering meaningful, compelling dialogue that is illuminating not just for Muslims, but also non-Muslims seeking to learn more about gender issues in Islam.

The Muslim Community Must Define Itself

Altmuslimah's contributors argue passionately for what they believe and the comments section is always alive with constructive feedback and sincere attempts at dealing with tough issues and finding workable solutions. Altmuslimah is, in this sense, uniquely probing. Its readers and contributors rarely engage in identity politics, instead focusing on a clear articulation of Muslim beliefs and socio-spiritual experiences. By taking control of their own narratives, Altmuslimah's writers make it less likely that others may attribute motives to them. They are sincere, but not apologetic, and are ultimately comfortable with disagreement.

In the coming century, the Muslim community in the U.S. and abroad will be faced with challenges that require a concerted and critical response. There is a great burden on community leaders to meet these challenges with an eye to the future, rather than simply predicating current behavior on past examples. A burden of proof has been placed on the Muslim community to prove that its religious tenets stand up to the scrutiny of international human rights standards. In addition to a general mistrust of the perceived heritage of such standards, variant interpretations of Islam and conflicting cultural identities complicate such a task. To adequately meet the challenges ahead, the Muslim community must be willing to actively and openly engage both its members as well as outside communities. The Muslim community must not be afraid to ask the question, *"What does it mean to be a Muslim today?"*

"In countries where the Church wields considerable power, the repercussions for women's lives are palpable."

The Catholic Church Limits Women's and Reproductive Rights

Nancy Northup

In the following viewpoint, a women's health-care advocate argues that the Catholic Church's position against abortion and contraception has led to the denial of basic human rights to women in many countries. She points out examples of the struggles faced by women globally, from unsafe abortion to children suffering from poverty and malnourishment, showing that the Church's supposed goal of assisting the poor and marginalized is often undermined by its stance on women's reproductive health care. Nancy Northup is the president of the Center for Reproductive Rights.

As you read, consider the following questions:

1. As stated by the author, what methods of abortion do Kenyan women engage in due to the fact that the act is criminalized in that country?

Human Rights

2. How many Filipino women have unsafe abortions every year, according to Northup?
3. What choices does the author believe help women to thrive?

O pinion pages of U.S. newspapers lambasted a decision by St. Joseph's Hospital, a Catholic institution in Phoenix, over the excommunication and demotion of a nun. Sister Margaret McBride was a head administrator at St. Joseph's Hospital who compassionately granted a critically ill young woman permission to have an abortion because continuing the pregnancy posed an immediate and grave risk to her life.

While many focused on the Church's "automatic excommunication" of McBride, an action squarely within the Church's religious purview, only a few addressed the secular punishment—her demotion from head administrator. In that action, the St. Joseph's Hospital was acting as a provider to the public of essential health care. As such, it should not be able to penalize an employee who acted within legal boundaries to deliver life-saving medical care, nor should it be permitted to withhold needed care for those who find themselves in its hospital wings. Indeed, a decision to let the young woman die instead would have been medical negligence as well as a grave violation of her legal and human rights.

The St. Joseph's story is, sadly, unsurprising. As human rights lawyers who work around the globe, we repeatedly confront the tragic consequences of the Catholic Church's sustained hostility to reproductive health services when it imposes its theology on public policy and the provision of health services to the public. In countries where the Church wields considerable power, the repercussions for women's lives are palpable.

Women Suffer When the Catholic Church Is in Control

In Kenya, for example, Catholic leaders are currently threatening to scuttle the adoption of a new constitution—widely seen as

176

The Catholic Campaign Against Emergency Contraception

The Catholic campaign against emergency contraception has made it unavailable in most Catholic hospitals, even when this hospital is the only one available in the area and the person requesting emergency contraception is not a Catholic. The most brutal example of Catholic clerical insensitivity to women is its opposition to the distribution of emergency contraception to refugee women of Kosovo who had fled to the camps after having been raped in the war [the 1999 Kosovo War in which various ethnic groups fought for control of the region, a part of the former Yugoslavia]. This view of the woman made pregnant by rape in war is also illustrated by the appeal in 1993 by Pope John Paul II to Bosnian Muslim women who had been raped [during the Bosnian War (1992–1995) that also followed the breakup of Yugoslavia] to turn their rape into an act of love by 'accepting the enemy into them' and carrying their pregnancies to term.

Rosemary Radford Ruether, "Women,
Reproductive Rights and the Catholic Church,"
Feminist Theology, *2008.*

critical to ending political bloodshed there—because it contains a clause on abortion. The provision in fact would forbid abortion except in emergencies or when a woman's life or health is in danger. But the Church would prefer to preserve the narrower exceptions on the books today, which criminalize abortion except to save the woman's life. Poverty, a dearth of sexuality education, and sexual violence all fuel an epidemic of unintended pregnancy. Ultimately, Kenyan women ingest bleach, detergent, or other dangerous liquids, insert sharp objects or resort to back-alley abortions. Every year, tens of thousands die or suffer debilitating damage to their health.

In Europe, the Catholic hierarchy has become especially effective in some former Eastern Bloc countries, resulting in backsliding on access to reproductive health services. In 2008, when a Catholic priest in a Polish town found out that a 14-year-old girl was seeking an abortion (for grounds legal under Polish law), he unleashed a campaign of harassment against her and her mother. They were besieged by protests, phone calls, and text messages. The priest cornered the girl alone in her hospital room in an attempt to convince her to continue her pregnancy. He then helped persuade authorities to take her away from her parents and place her in a state-run juvenile center. The girl and her mother are now suing Poland in the European Court of Human Rights. It's the fourth abortion-related case against Poland in the court that we've been involved in over the last six years.

The Philippines, where the government is closely tied to the Catholic hierarchy, provides another example. Not only is abortion criminalized with no clear exceptions, but due to the Church's influence, the government strongly discourages contraception. In Manila, an order by the mayor pulled every birth control pill and condom off the shelves of public health facilities, and forbade even sterilization.

For the population in Manila, most who live below the poverty line, the policy banning modern methods of contraception causes irreparable damage. It's not uncommon to see families with six or more severely malnourished children, living in one-room shacks surrounded by garbage and streams of sewage, and facing very few prospects for relief. Understandably, without access to affordable contraception, over half-a-million Filipino women in desperate circumstances turn to unsafe abortion each year. As in Kenya, the methods are crude and painful, and the subsequent deaths and complications suffered by women can only be described as a public health crisis.

This year at home, we saw the U.S. government give the Conference of Catholic Bishops veto power over the health-care reform bill, and in the end, millions of American women were left with a policy that restricts insurance coverage for abortion services even for those who pay for their insurance with their own hard-earned dollars.

The Catholic Church Must Uphold Human Rights in the Public Arena

The Catholic Church promises to serve the interests of the poor and marginalized, but its position on reproductive health is deeply at odds with those laudable goals. Societies thrive when women thrive—when they are able to finish their education, decide the number and spacing of their children, and live in dignity and equality. Depriving women of the ability to control their reproductive health and fertility does not create a moral and just world. It only further traps women, their families, and their communities in poverty and despair.

The Catholic Church, like any religion, is sovereign in the realm of its theology, liturgy, practice, and requirements of membership. But when it chooses to provide health services to the public as in the case of Saint Joseph's Hospital, or enters the realm of public policy debates in Kenya, the Philippines, Poland or the U.S., the governing standard must be the basic human rights of women to control their health and lives.

> "Employers, employees, and issuers who have moral and religious objections to sterilization, contraception, and abortion are not free to have health care coverage that excludes these practices."

Legislative Mandates on Women's and Reproductive Rights Infringe on Religious Freedom

John Garvey

In the following viewpoint, a Catholic university president maintains that the recent passage of US health-care legislation requiring the delivery of certain types of reproductive health-care services threatens to infringe upon individuals' ability to freely exercise their right to refrain from participating in the provision of these types of care. He insists that any health-care bill requiring reproductive health care must include a conscience clause that allows individuals who oppose certain methods, such as abortion or contraception, on religious grounds to abstain from delivering it without fear of suffering punishment. John Garvey is the president of the Catholic University of America.

As you read, consider the following questions:

1. What does the Church Amendment protect, as stated by Garvey?

2. According to the author, what are some of the reproduction and contraceptive services that the Institute of Medicine suggested the Department of Health and Human Services cover?

3. Upon what grounds does the author base his claim that it is important to include a conscience clause in health-care laws?

About four months after he became president, George Washington had an exchange of letters with a group of Quakers in five states. They had written him for some assurances that the new government would protect their religious liberty. Here is what our first president said in reply:

> I assure you very explicitly, that in my opinion the conscientious scruples of all men should be treated with great delicacy and tenderness: and it is my wish and desire, that the laws may always be as extensively accommodated to them, as a due regard for the protection and essential interests of the nation may justify and permit.

This assurance extended even to the Quakers' refusal to fight in the military, an exemption that the commander-in-chief acknowledged with some grumbling. I think it is a point of pride for Americans that, even with the differences we have had recently over many issues of health care, we adhere so carefully to Washington's promise of conscientious accommodation. For almost 40 years the Church Amendment has protected conscientious objection to abortion and sterilization where federal funds are involved. For 25 years our foreign aid programs for family planning have said that "no applicant shall be discriminated against because of [a] conscientious commitment to offer only natural family planning." In the District of Columbia, where I live, Congress has stipulated for more than a decade that "any legislation enacted [to mandate contraceptive coverage] should include a 'conscience clause' which provides exceptions for religious beliefs and moral convictions." The 2003 Act for United States Leadership Against HIV/AIDS gives religious organizations a right to participate fully, and promises that they need not "participate in any program or activity to which the organization has a religious or moral objection."

New Health-Care Legislation Threatens Conscientious Objections to Contraception

I worry that this distinguished record of liberal toleration might soon come to an end. The Patient Protection and Affordable Care Act authorizes the Department of Health and Human Services [HHS] to draw up new lists of "preventive services for women" that must be included in private health plans. Last week the Institute of Medicine (a nonprofit organization; it's the health arm of the National Academy of Sciences) issued a set of recommendations to HHS about what such preventive services might comprise. Though the Institute might have addressed many important issues, it focused mainly on reproduction and contraception. It suggested that HHS mandate coverage of surgical sterilization, all FDA [Food and Drug Administration]-approved prescription contraceptives (including drugs like Ella that are targeted at women who may already have conceived), and "education and counseling" to promote these services. HHS will decide soon (perhaps as early as August 1 [2011]) whether to adopt these recommendations.

Americans differ over whether the services recommended by the Institute of Medicine are bad things. But the issue before HHS is not whether to allow sterilization, contraception, and abortion. It is whether to order insurance companies to cover these services, and employers and employees to pay for them, even if they view them as morally wrong. It is in just this situation that the respect for religious freedom comes into play. Most Americans view service in the armed forces, especially in times of trouble, as a good thing. Most are willing to sanction even the taking of enemy lives, if it is necessary to protect our country and those we love. Quakers do not, and from the beginning of our history we have treated their "conscientious scruples . . . with great delicacy and tenderness."

Health-Care Mandates Must Not Infringe on Rights of Conscience

It is unfortunate that the new health care law enacted in 2010 does not include a conscience clause addressing this issue. But it is natural and appropriate that HHS should consider our historical commitment to religious liberty in deciding what kinds of services to mandate. The administration promised that Americans who like their current health care coverage could keep it after we enacted the new reform. Employers, employees, and issuers who have moral and religious objections to sterilization, contraception, and abortion are now free to have health care coverage that excludes these practices. It would break both old and new promises to deprive them of that liberty.

I hope HHS does the right thing in considering the Institute's proposals. If it does not, Reps. Jeff Fortenberry (R-NE) and Dan Boren (D-OK) have introduced the Respect for Rights of Conscience Act (H.R. 1179) to address the absence of a conscience clause in the Patient Protection and Affordable Care Act. The bill would prevent any new mandates introduced to implement the health care act from infringing upon the rights of conscience that Americans currently enjoy. It is a measure that everyone who cares about religious liberty can support.

Periodical and Internet Sources Bibliography

The following articles have been chosen to supplement the diverse views presented in this chapter.

Robert Carle   "Revealing and Concealing:
                        Islamist Discourse on Human
                        Rights," *Human Rights Review*,
                        April–June 2005.

Douglas Farrow   "The Audacity of the State,"
                        *Touchstone: A Journal of Mere
                        Christianity*, January 2010.

Luis Granados   "Strategies for Fighting Blasphemy
                        Laws in a Post-Tolerant World,"
                        Humanist, May–June 2010.

Edmund C. Hurlbutt   "Abortion 'Rights' and the Duty
                        Not to Know," *Human Life Review*,
                        Summer 2011.

Mick MacAndrew   "When Freedom of Religion
                        Trumps Free Speech," *Eureka
                        Street*, August 14, 2009.

Khaleel Mohammed   "A Muslim Perspective on Human
                        Rights," *Society*, January–February
                        2004.

Dallin H. Oaks   "In Defense of Religious Freedom,"
                        Vital Speeches of the Day, January
                        2010.

George Pell   "The Struggle for Religious
                        Freedom," *Quadrant Magazine*,
                        January 2010.

Lise Storm   "The Dilemma of the Islamists:
                        Human Rights, Democratization
                        and the War on Terror," *Middle
                        East Policy*, Spring 2009.

Mariz Tadros   "Introduction: Gender, Rights and
                        Religion at the Crossroads," *IDS
                        Bulletin*, January 2011.

Daniel Wehrenfennig   "The Human Right of Religious
                        Freedom in International Law,"
                        Peace Review, July–September
                        2006.

OPPOSING
VIEWPOINTS®
SERIES

CHAPTER 4

Are All Rights Human Rights?

Chapter Preface

Human rights are generally understood to be those rights that must be afforded to any person simply because he or she is human. The United Nations Universal Declaration of Human Rights (UDHR), signed in 1948, helped to establish a more concrete definition of specific rights that fall under this definition. However, even with the signing of this document, many questions remain about what rights should be considered human rights. For example, according to Article 25 of the UDHR, "Everyone has the right to a standard of living adequate for the health and well-being of himself and of his family, including food, clothing, housing and medical care and necessary social services." While there is little debate over whether individuals should be able to freely seek the necessary goods and services to fulfill this right, the government's role in guaranteeing access to these goods and services is not entirely clear. In the United States, attempts to determine if the government is responsible for providing health care to those who cannot afford it have led to disputes about whether health care should be defined as a human right.

Many advocates of universal health care in the United States have cited the UDHR to support their claims that access to health care qualifies as a human right that should be provided to those who cannot afford it. In supporting its calls for US health-care reform, the human rights organization Amnesty International contends, "Everyone has the right to health, including health care, according to the Universal Declaration of Human Rights. Health care is a public good, not a commodity." The National Economic and Social Rights Initiative maintains that when health care is treated as a commodity it creates a system that "sells access to health care based on a person's ability to pay rather than their health needs," thus creating an unequal and unsustainable system that leaves millions without access to a basic human right.

While many who view health care as a human right oppose its commodification, others maintain more people have access when health care is not regulated by the government. In the article "What 'Right' to Health Care?" *Boston Globe* columnist Jeff Jacoby compares health care to food and clothing, identifying all three as "essential to human welfare." He states, "It may seem noble to declare that health care is a fundamental human right and not a mere commodity to be left to the vagaries of the market. . . . [However] it is precisely because food and clothing *are* seen as commodities . . . that they can be had in such abundance and diversity." In this view, health care should not be treated as a human right because doing so would define it as a public good, not a commodity, and remove it from the free market sphere, thus constraining accessibility, not enhancing it.

The question of whether health care should be considered a human right is only one controversy within the larger discussion about what rights can be defined as human rights. In the following chapter, authors contest whether water and Internet access should be considered human rights and how that label would impact accessibility.

| "The lack of access to clean water and sanitation, in terms of sheer numbers affected, is arguably the single biggest human rights issue of our time."

Access to Water Is an Inalienable Human Right

Maude Barlow

In the following viewpoint, a Canadian activist contends that access to water and sanitation must be viewed as a basic human right and protected fervently by government and international organizations worldwide. She argues that when people do not have access to clean water, they are unable to pursue happy, healthy lives, and in millions of cases, die from waterborne disease. Maude Barlow is the national chairperson of the citizen advocacy organization, the Council of Canadians, and co-founder of the Blue Planet Project, which works to ensure the human right to water is guaranteed worldwide.

As you read, consider the following questions:

1. How often does a child in the developing world die of a waterborne disease, according to the Bolivian UN ambassador quoted by the author?

Maude Barlow, *Our Right to Water: A People's Guide to Implementing the United Nations' Recognition of the Right to Water and Sanitation.* Ottawa, Ontario: The Council of Canadians, June 2011. Copyright © 2011 by the Council of Canadians. All rights reserved. Reproduced by permission.

2. What four issues does Barlow identify as having contributed to the problem of inaccessibility to water and sanitation, particularly in the developing world?
3. According to the UN survey cited by the author, how many hours do women in developing countries spend collecting water?

On July 28, 2010, the United Nations General Assembly adopted an historic resolution recognizing the human right to safe and clean drinking water and sanitation as "essential for the full enjoyment of the right to life." For those of us in the balcony of the General Assembly that day, the air was tense with suspense. A number of powerful countries had lined up to oppose the resolution so it had to be put to a vote. Bolivian UN Ambassador Pablo Solón introduced the resolution by reminding the Assembly that human bodies are made up of almost two-thirds of water and that our blood flows like a network of rivers to transport nutrients and energy to our bodies. "Water is life," he said.

But then he laid out the tragic and growing numbers of people around the world dying from lack of access to clean water. He quoted a new World Health Organization study on diarrhoea showing that every three-and-a-half seconds in the developing world, a child dies of water-borne disease. Ambassador Solón then quietly snapped his fingers three times and held his small finger up for a half second. The General Assembly of the United Nations fell silent. Moments later, it voted overwhelmingly to recognize the human right to water and sanitation. People on the floor erupted in cheers.

Water and Sanitation Are Human Rights

Two months later, the UN Human Rights Council adopted a second resolution affirming that water and sanitation are human rights, adding that the human right to safe drinking water and sanitation is derived from the right to an adequate standard of living and is "inextricably related to the right to the highest attainable standard of physical and mental health as well as the right to life and human dignity." Together, the two resolutions represent an extraordinary breakthrough in the international struggle for the right to safe clean drinking water and sanitation and a crucial milestone in the fight for water justice. The resolutions also complete the promises of the 1992 Rio Earth Summit where water, climate change, biodiversity and desertification were all targeted for action. All but water had been addressed by the United Nations with a convention and a plan; the circle has finally closed. . . .

It is crucial to underline that the two resolutions do not *confer* new rights. The right to clean water and sanitation inherently exists for every person on Earth and for future generations. Rather, the new resolutions *recognize* these inherent rights and set out the obligations that States now carry in regard to clean water and sanitation. As well, while this [viewpoint] primarily deals with a human right, it is clear that it is not possible to protect the human right to water and sanitation without recognizing the inherent rights of nature and other species. Weaving the rights of nature into the interpretation of the "right to water" is essential for true transformation. Similarly, the genuine realization of these new rights will require recognizing and honouring that some cultures place responsibility and relationship of community over the more "western" notion of individual rights. Promoting respect for the traditional and collective values of a diversity of cultures will strengthen the reach of the human right to water and sanitation internationally and expand the possibilities for its application. . . .

Consumption and Pollution Depleted World Water Supplies

Water was not included in the 1948 Universal Declaration of Human Rights because, at the time, no one could perceive of a world lacking in clean water. All over the world, people learned that there is a finite and specific amount of water that circulates through the hydrologic cycle and that it cannot be destroyed. So humans wantonly polluted, mismanaged and displaced water as if it was indestructible, using it to grow crops in deserts, dump as waste in oceans, and send out of watersheds in the form of virtual water exports to support a global market economy.

Using borewell technology that did not exist a hundred years ago, humans have relentlessly mined groundwater at an alarming rate. Worldwide overpumping of groundwater more than doubled between 1960 and 2000 and is responsible for about 25 percent of the rise in sea levels. A recent study on the global water supply conducted by water intensive industries and coordinated by the World Bank found that by 2030, global demand for water will exceed supply by 40 percent. The world's rivers, the single largest renewable water resource for humans and a crucible of aquatic biodiversity, are in a crisis of ominous proportions. The journal *Nature* reports that nearly 80 percent of the world's human population lives in areas where river waters are highly threatened, posing a major threat to human water security.

As well as massively robbing watersheds of their water, humans have also relentlessly polluted them. In many parts of the world, surface and groundwater are contaminated and completely unsafe for drinking, cooking and fishing. In the Global South [nations of Africa, Central and Latin America, and parts of Asia], more than 90 percent of sewage and 70 percent of industrial wastewater is dumped untreated into surface water. Every day, two million tons (almost 2 billion kilograms) of sewage and industrial waste are discharged into the world's water, the equivalent of the weight of the entire human population of 6.8 billion people. The amount of wastewater produced annually is about six times more water than exists in all the rivers of the world.

Poverty and Commodification Make Water Inaccessible

These two crises of declining water and poisoned water sources are extremely concerning on their own; but when combined with a world of people with increasing class and income disparities, these crises are lethal. By every measurement, global income disparities are more severe than they have been in almost a century. A small percentage of the world's elite owns the vast majority of assets. Billions of people around the world live in poverty amongst great wealth and this affects their access to water. A child born in the developed world consumes 30 to 50 times more water than one in the developing world. Peri-urban slums ring most of the developing world's cities where climate and food refugees are arriving in relentless numbers. Unable to access their traditional sources of water either because they have disappeared or have been polluted, and unable to afford high water rates set by newly privatized water services, these refugees must rely on sources contaminated by their own untreated human waste as well as industrial poisons for drinking water.

The growing commodification of the world's water has made it increasingly inaccessible to those without money. Many poor countries have been strongly encouraged by the World Bank to contract water services to private for-profit utilities, a practice that has spawned fierce resistance by millions of people left out due to poverty. Other struggles are taking place with bottled water companies that drain local water supplies, very often in poor and indigenous communities. There are "land grabs" where countries and investment funds buy up massive amounts of land in the Global South for access to the water and soil for future use. Some countries actually auction off water to global interests, such as mining companies, which now literally own the water that used to belong to rural communities and local farmers. And many countries are introducing water markets and water trading, whereby a water licence, often owned by private companies or industrial agribusiness, is converted to property to be hoarded, bought, sold and traded, sometimes on the open international market, to those who can afford to buy it. In all of these cases, water becomes the private property of those with the means to buy it and is increasingly denied to those without. All over the world, small farmers, peasants, indigenous people and the poor have found themselves unable to stand up to these private interests. As the operations of the water companies became more global, backed by global financial institutions, it became clear that nation/state instruments alone were no longer sufficient to protect citizens. . . .

Water Access Is the Most Significant Human Rights Issue

Meanwhile, all over the Global South, and increasingly in poor communities in the Global North, those who cannot pay for the vanishing supplies of clean water are getting sick and dying. As Ambassador Solón reported when he spoke to the UN General Assembly, every year, 3.5 million people die of waterborne disease; half the hospital beds on Earth are occupied by people suffering from waterborne disease; more than 1 billion people lack access to potable water; and 2.6 billion people have no access to the dignity of basic sanitation. Aaron Wolf, program director in Water Conflict and Management and Transformation at Oregon State University says, "The current water crisis is bigger than the crises brought on by HIV/AIDs, malaria, tsunamis, earthquakes and all of the wars in a given year."

The situation is hardest on women and children. A 2006 United Nations survey carried out in 177 countries revealed that women spend about 40 billion hours collecting water every year. In many countries, women spend as much as five or six hours each day fetching water and their female children accompany them, keeping them out of school. In every case, if these families had money, the children would not be dying and would be attending school. The lack of access to clean water and sanitation, in terms of sheer numbers affected, is arguably the single biggest human rights issue of our time. Without the recognition of this right, and the obligations it places on governments to find a solution that is supported by adequate financial resources, the suffering will only deepen. . . .

The Right to Water Is Only the First Step

When the United Nations recognized the human right to water and sanitation, humanity took a collective step forward in its evolution. But this alone is not enough. The dominant economic system of unbridled, unregulated market capitalism and unlimited growth has brought the planet to the brink of an ecological crisis and created income disparities and economic injustice unparalleled in recent history. We now face a situation of extreme concentration of economic and resource power, which has led to both environmental degradation and the social, economic and environmental exclusion of the majority of the world's people. No recognition of the right to water and sanitation can alone deliver water and sanitation to the billions living without them as long as this system goes unchallenged.

To truly implement the spirit of the right to water and sanitation for all, we must confront the current economic system and work to create new economic, social and resource policies based on the principles of inclusion, equity, diversity, sustainability, and democracy. We need to promote local sustainable food production practices, local sustainable goods production, and a conversion from fossil fuels to safe, alternative energy sources. Economic structures should be designed to move economic and political power downward, toward the local, rather than the global, and the power of transnational corporations and speculation capital must be constrained and brought under the rule of law. The rush to privatize every area once considered a common heritage must end.

Water Is a Public Good

To truly share the world's water sources in an equitable and responsible way, we must recognize water as a shared common heritage to be fiercely protected, carefully managed, and equitably shared. Because it is a flow resource necessary for life and ecosystem health, and because there is no substitute for it, water must be regarded as a public commons and a public good and preserved as such for all time in law and practice. Freshwater is central to our very existence and must be protected by public trust law for the common good, not for individual profit. Of course there is an economic dimension to water, but under the public trust, governments are obliged to protect water sources in order to sustain them for the long-term use of the entire population, not just the privileged few. This will require taking water out of all trade and investment agreements and removing the power of corporations to sue governments under these agreements if governments move to constrain corporate activity in order to protect watersheds and water supplies.

Another imperative to ensure the right to water and sanitation is to challenge the market-driven development paradigm and place human rights-based approaches resistant to the dominance of free-market ideology at the heart of all development work. Ellen Dorsey of the Wallace Foundation notes that this would ensure the meaningful participation of people affected by development programs, address the root causes of poverty, discrimination and exclusion, and give the most marginalized communities priority in law and practice. She suggests renaming the Millennium Development Goals, Millennium Development Rights.

The Right to Water Must Lead to an Expansion of Other Rights

As we move to define and expand the notion of the right to water and sanitation, we also need to explore ways to enlarge the definition of rights to include third generation rights, such as the right to self-determination, group and collective rights, and the right to local natural resources. In doing so, we would be recognizing the concerns of many cultural and traditional communities that the UN rights-based system may be limited to a more Western notion of individual rights at the expense of other, more collective ways of advancing human rights. The United

Nations Declaration on the Rights of Indigenous Peoples is an excellent example of third generation rights in that it includes among its stated rights: self-determination; distinct political, legal, economic, social, cultural and spiritual institutions; traditional knowledge; dignity and well-being; conservation and protection of natural resources on indigenous territory; and free and informed consent on any resource project affecting them. The definition of human rights is not static, much as some would like to have it rigidly and narrowly defined. The issue of water and sanitation offers us an excellent opportunity to explore this notion of rights that one day, will extend to water itself.

To ensure that there will be adequate supplies of clean accessible water for all, we will eventually need to create a body of law for the natural world. In the eyes of most Western law most of the community of life on Earth remains mere "property," and water is increasingly seen as another commodity to be exploited. Modern humans tend to see water as a resource for our pleasure, convenience and profit and not as the essential element in a living ecosystem that gives us all life. We need to develop laws and practices to protect water, outside its usefulness to humans, and to restore and permanently protect watersheds and water sources. We need to adopt laws, like Ecuador has done, asserting that natural communities and ecosystems possess the inalienable right to exist, flourish and evolve, and, as much as possible, leave water where it is, understanding its vital role in nourishing ecosystems and protecting the healthy functioning of the hydrologic cycle. We cannot build a body of rights for humans without the corresponding body of rights for the Earth and other species. To this end, it is crucial to support the campaign to have the UN adopt the Universal Declaration on the Rights of Mother Earth to eventually serve as the companion to the Universal Declaration of Human Rights.

"Water is not equally distributed,
leading to insufficient access."

Fundamental Human Need

Business Recorder

In the viewpoint that follows, the Business Recorder *discusses the background to the water crises and the difficulties of gaining access to clean drinking water. These difficulties include poverty, power relationships, and contaminated drinking sources. According to the viewpoint, due to a lack of statistics, the number of people without water access is underestimated. Although these conflicts exist, the UN General Assembly has declared clean water as a human right. The* Business Recorder *is a financial news daily based in Pakistan.*

As you read, consider the following questions:

1. What are the estimated numbers of people who lack access to safe drinking water and who lack access to basic sanitation, as reported in the viewpoint?
2. According to the viewpoint, what portion of the total water used worldwide is for personal and domestic use?
3. Why are the number of residents and the status of water provision in informal urban settlements unknown?

On 28 July 2010 General Assembly declares that the safe and clean drinking water and sanitation is a human right essential to the full enjoyment of life and all other human rights. The 192-member Assembly also called on United Nations Member States and international organisations to offer funding, technology and other resources to help poorer countries scale up their efforts to provide clean, accessible and affordable drinking water and sanitation for everyone.

It is now time to consider access to safe drinking water and sanitation as a human right, defined as the right to equal and non-discriminatory access to a sufficient amount of safe drinking water for personal and domestic uses—drinking, personal sanitation, washing of clothes, food preparation and personal and household hygiene—to sustain life and health. States should prioritise these personal and domestic uses over other water uses and should take steps to ensure that this sufficient amount is of good quality, affordable for all and can be collected within a reasonable distance from a person's home.

An estimated 884 million people lack access to safe drinking water and a total of more than 2.6 billion people do not have access to basic sanitation.

Studies also indicate about 1.5 million children under the age of five die each year due to water borne diseases.

443 million school days are lost because of water- and sanitation-related diseases.

Right to Water: Context of the Water Crisis

The world contains sufficient, clean freshwater for everyone's basic personal and domestic needs. Personal and domestic uses of water account for less than ten per cent of the total amount of water used in human activities, although essential uses require a significantly lower percentage.

The View of Water as a Commodity

At the risk of over-simplification, the commodity view asserts that private ownership and management of water supply systems (in distinction from water itself) is possible and indeed preferable. From this perspective, water is no different than other essential goods and utility services. Private companies, who will be responsive both to customers and to shareholders, can efficiently run and profitably manage water supply systems. Commercialization rescripts water as an economic good rather than a public good, and redefines users as individual customers rather than a collective of citizens. Water conservation can thus be incentivized through pricing—users will cease wasteful behaviour as water prices rise with increasing scarcity. Proponents of the "commodity" view assert that water must be treated as an economic good, as specified in the Dublin Principles and in the Hague Declaration, similar to any other economic good—such as food—essential for life.

Karen Bakker, "The 'Commons' versus the 'Commodity': Alter-Globalization, Anti-Privatization and the Human Right to Water in The Global South," Antipode, June 2007.

However, water is not equally distributed, leading to insufficient access. Lack of distribution networks, working systems to extract groundwater or harvest rainwater and, in some cases, exclusion from these services or facilities, limit the extent of peoples access to sufficient water. In some cases, excessive extraction of groundwater, often for agricultural or industrial use, limits domestic use and threatens the long-term sustainability of such groundwater sources. Groundwater is also at increasing risk of contamination from untreated wastewater from agriculture, industry or households.

The 2006 UNDP Human Development Report stresses that issues related to poverty, inequality and unequal power relationships cause the current water and sanitation crisis. At the time, over 1.1 billion individuals lacked access to a basic supply of water from a clean source that is likely to be safe; of these, the majority are people living in rural areas, according to the WHO UNICEF Joint Monitoring Programme. The figure of 1.1 billion does not include the number of people who are unable to afford water, who face prohibitive waiting times for collecting water, who receive water at occasional intervals or have to collect water from dangerous areas.

In rural areas, many people collect water of dubious quality from unprotected wells or surface water sources, often at a great distance from their homes, deterring them from collecting sufficient quantities. This problem is significantly worse during the dry season, when the water table drops, and rivers and shallow wells dry up.

In urban areas, low-income groups, in particular those living in informal settlements, will often lack access to an adequate water supply and sanitation. Piped supplies seldom cover informal areas, meaning that people living there access water from a variety of generally inadequate water supply options, such as wells built close to latrines, water kiosks with water of dubious origin or from water vendors.

Due to a lack of adequate statistics, the number of people without access to water is often underestimated. As many of the informal settlements in urban areas are unrecognised by the local or national governments, the exact number of residents living in these settlements is often unknown, as is the status of water provision. Tenants may also be missing from the statistics where landlords do not declare them. Water can also be prohibitively expensive, so that even where water is available, people do not have access to a sufficient quantity for health and hygiene practices. As a result, there is considerable inequality in distribution of water and sanitation services in urban areas, with smaller urban centers particularly badly affected. Statistics for access to water and sanitation services in urban areas therefore tend to be uneven. Further to this, while people may use safe sources of water for some of their purposes, such as for drinking, this source may be prohibitively expensive to use for all domestic uses, forcing people to use unsafe sources for washing or cooking. This is not reflected in the statistics of access to water supply.

> *"It is a mistake to put any particular technology in this exalted category [of human rights], since over time we will end up valuing the wrong things."*

Internet Access Is Not a Human Right

Vinton G. Cerf

In the following viewpoint, a US computer scientist contends that Internet access cannot be considered a human right. While he concedes that the Internet can be a powerful tool in helping people maintain and improve their human rights, he makes a sharp distinction between a human right and an enabler of human rights. Further, he maintains that because technology is constantly changing, granting one specific technology the status of a human right would wrongly emphasize the importance of one technology that will likely change or perhaps become obsolete in the future. Vinton G. Cerf is hailed as one of the "fathers of the Internet."

As you read, consider the following questions:

1. What are two countries identified by Cerf that have designated Internet access as a human right?

2. As stated by Cerf, how is granting Internet access the status of a human right like granting horse ownership the status of a human right?
3. Why is it more plausible to consider Internet access a civil right as opposed to a human right, according to the author?

From the streets of Tunis [the capital of Tunisia] to Tahrir Square [in Cairo, Egypt] and beyond, protests around the world last year [2011] were built on the Internet and the many devices that interact with it. Though the demonstrations thrived because thousands of people turned out to participate, they could never have happened as they did without the ability that the Internet offers to communicate, organize and publicize everywhere, instantaneously.

It is no surprise, then, that the protests have raised questions about whether Internet access is or should be a civil or human right. The issue is particularly acute in countries whose governments clamped down on Internet access in an attempt to quell the protesters. In June, citing the uprisings in the Middle East and North Africa, a report by the United Nations' special rapporteur went so far as to declare that the Internet had "become an indispensable tool for realizing a range of human rights." Over the past few years, courts and parliaments in countries like France and Estonia have pronounced Internet access a human right.

Technology Is an Enabler Not a Right

But that argument, however well meaning, misses a larger point: technology is an enabler of rights, not a right itself. There is a high bar for something to be considered a human right. Loosely put, it must be among the things we as humans need in order to lead healthy, meaningful lives, like freedom from torture or freedom of conscience. It is a mistake to place any particular technology in this exalted category, since over time we will end up valuing the wrong things. For example, at one time if you didn't have a horse it was hard to make a living. But the important right in that case was the right to make a living, not the right to a horse. Today, if I were granted a right to have a horse, I'm not sure where I would put it.

The best way to characterize human rights is to identify the outcomes that we are trying to ensure. These include critical freedoms like freedom of speech and freedom of access to information—and those are not necessarily bound to any particular technology at any particular time. Indeed, even the United Nations report, which was widely hailed as declaring Internet access a human right, acknowledged that the Internet was valuable as a means to an end, not as an end in itself.

What about the claim that Internet access is or should be a *civil* right? The same reasoning above can be applied here—Internet access is always just a tool for obtaining something else more important—though the argument that it is a civil right is, I concede, a stronger one than that it is a human right. Civil rights, after all, are different from human rights because they are conferred upon us by law, not intrinsic to us as human beings.

While the United States has never decreed that everyone has a "right" to a telephone, we have come close to this with the notion of "universal service"—the idea that telephone service (and electricity, and now broadband Internet) must be available even in the most remote regions of the country. When we accept this idea, we are edging into the idea of Internet access as a civil right, because ensuring access is a policy made by the government.

Technology Creators Must Be Mindful of Human Rights

Yet all these philosophical arguments overlook a more fundamental issue: the responsibility of technology creators themselves to support human and civil rights. The Internet has introduced an enormously accessible and egalitarian platform for creating, sharing and obtaining information on a global scale. As a result, we have new ways to allow people to exercise their human and civil rights.

In this context, engineers have not only a tremendous obligation to empower users, but also an obligation to ensure the safety of users online. That means, for example, protecting users from specific harms like viruses and worms that silently invade their computers. Technologists should work toward this end.

It is engineers—and our professional associations and standards-setting bodies like the Institute of Electrical and Electronics Engineers—that create and maintain these new capabilities. As we seek to advance the state of the art in technology and its use in society, we must be conscious of our civil responsibilities in addition to our engineering expertise.

Improving the Internet is just one means, albeit an important one, by which to improve the human condition. It must be done with an appreciation for the civil and human rights that deserve protection—without pretending that access itself is such a right.

"Downplaying the importance and amazing abilities of the Internet to improve the human condition is dangerous."

Internet Access Is a Human Right

JD Rucker

In the following viewpoint, a social media strategist argues that access to the Internet should be considered a basic human right. He views the Internet as a means for people to improve their society and believes that those without Internet access have a disadvantage when it comes to their ability to live happy and prosperous lives. Under these two conditions, he maintains that Internet access must be considered a human right because its denial leaves those who are without less able to fulfill their human potential. JD Rucker is an editor for Soshable, a social media marketing blog.

As you read, consider the following questions:

1. What three questions does Rucker ask to determine whether Internet access should be considered a human right?
2. How has the Internet influenced people fighting oppression, according to the author?

3. As stated by the author, how is Internet access similar to access to medication?

Technology and philosophy have been at the center of more debates lately than ever before. It's clear that technology is advancing faster than anyone would have imagined a decade ago, while an argument could be made that the philosophies that brought the world this far are starting to regress to less-civilized times. In the question of whether or not Internet access is a human right or simply a privilege, technology and philosophy collide dramatically.

The arguments that Vinton G. Cerf, Google's Chief Internet Evangelist and a prominent computer scientist recognized as a "father of the Internet," makes in his article titled "Internet Access Is Not a Human Right" are quite compelling. He states that "technology is an enabler of rights, not a right itself."

It's a "gotcha" statement that sidesteps the perception of those fighting for more Internet rights based upon the tremendous role the web played in uprisings in the Middle East and North Africa. In essence, his statement and the whole article attempts to reason with supporters of the United Nations report that declares Internet access is indeed, a human right. He acknowledges that the Internet was critical but that calling it a human right or even a civil right is taking it too far.

I disagree.

Human Rights Are Clearly Defined

There's no need to try to redefine what "human rights" are. According to Wikipedia, human rights are "commonly understood as inalienable fundamental rights to which a person is inherently entitled simply because she or he is a human being."

This fits in well today just as it fit when the term was introduced in the 18th century. The question really comes down to delivery of rights. Rather than trying to play around with semantics, we should be looking at the results of the last couple of years and make the determination based upon three questions:

1. Is it possible in the near future to create an infrastructure that would make *Internet access* available to nearly everyone in the world?
2. Would making *Internet access* available worldwide to the vast majority of people foster positive changes in every culture and every society?
3. Are those without *Internet access* less able to prosper?

The answer to number 1 is definitely yes, though not without challenges. Number 2 is debatable but recent history would have most leaning towards the affirmative. Number 3 is a personal philosophical question, but again the general perception is also affirmative here.

Technology is an enabler as Cerf states. In many cases, it's also a right; the two statuses are not mutually exclusive. He uses the example that owning a horse once made making a living easier, where the horse was the enabler and making a living was the human right. Technology is not a horse. The Internet is not a horse. Only a small percentage of people owned a horse while a large percentage were able to make a living.

Tools Are Necessary to Ensure Rights

It's not a coincidence that there seems to be a new uprising against oppression around the world every other month. Oppression isn't new. The desire to end oppression isn't new. The ability to organize, communicate, and learn using the Internet is the only thing that has been added to the equation. There have been more successful uprisings against powerful government entities in the last two years than in the past 50 years prior.

Downplaying the importance and amazing abilities of the Internet to improve the human condition is dangerous. In this case, I'm siding with the United Nations (something that I don't do very often). Vaulting the Internet to the highest plateau as a true human right is the right step towards ending more than just

The UN Supports Internet Access as a Human Right

By explicitly providing that everyone has the right to express him or herself through any media, the Special Rapporteur underscores that article 19 of the Universal Declaration of Human Rights and the Covenant was drafted with foresight to include and to accommodate future technological developments through which individuals can exercise their right to freedom of expression. Hence, the framework of international human rights law remains relevant today and equally applicable to new communication technologies such as the Internet.

The right to freedom of opinion and expression is as much a fundamental right on its own accord as it is an "enabler" of other rights, including economic, social and cultural rights, such as the right to education and the right to take part in cultural life and to enjoy the benefits of scientific progress and its applications, as well as civil and political rights, such as the rights to freedom of association and assembly. Thus, by acting as a catalyst for individuals to exercise their right to freedom of opinion and expression, the Internet also facilitates the realization of a range of other human rights.

Frank La Rue, "Report of the Special Rapporteur on the Promotion and Protection of the Right to Freedom of Opinion and Expression," United Nations Human Rights Council, May 16, 2011.

oppression worldwide. It's a step towards increased opportunity, improved education, and the end of hostilities based upon ignorance. It's an element much like medicine that should fall into the same category.

As an exercise in comparison, take the words *Internet access* out of the three questions above and replace them with *access to medication*. Most would agree that access to medication is a human right, but even it has basically the same answers when inserted into those questions.

Number 1: yes, though not without challenges. Number 2: debatable but most would lean towards the affirmative. Number 3: personal with a general perception of affirmative.

The statement that Cerf is trying to make is that technology and the Internet are means to an end, not the ends themselves. He's correct. That doesn't mean that they should be considered human rights. On the contrary, the discovery that giving people a tool that they can use to dramatically improve their lives should be used to rally support for the goal of giving everyone everywhere the ability to use the most profound technological breakthrough in decades.

If the United Nations declaring that Internet access should be a human right is the way to make it a reality, then we shouldn't be tinkering with the semantics of the statement. We should be striving to make it a reality.

Periodical and Internet Sources Bibliography

The following articles have been chosen to supplement the diverse views presented in this chapter.

Taposik Banerjee	"Right to Water: Some Theoretical Issues," *Contemporary Issues and Ideas in Social Sciences,* June 2010.
Hillary Rodham Clinton	"Internet Freedom and Human Rights," *Issues in Science and Technology,* Spring 2012.
Rowan Cruft	"Are Property Rights Ever Basic Human Rights?," *British Journal of Politics and International Relations,* February 2011.
Olivier de Schutter	"The Emerging Human Right to Land," *International Community Law Review,* September 2010.
Jason T. Eberl, Eleanore D. Kinney, and Matthew J. Williams	"Foundation for a Natural Right to Health Care," *Journal of Medicine and Philosophy,* December 2011.
Alice Hlidkova	"One Minute with . . . Kosta Grammatis," *New Scientist,* January 22, 2011.
Arjun Kumar Khadka	"The Emergence of Water as a 'Human Right' on the World Stage: Challenges and Opportunities," *International Journal of Water Resources Development,* March 2010.
Fred Magdoff	"Food as a Commodity," *Monthly Review: An Independent Socialist Magazine,* January 2012.
Fatima Measham	"Blogs and Monsters," *Eureka Street,* June 17, 2011.
Anna F.S. Russell	"International Organizations and Human Rights: Realizing, Resisting or Repackaging the Right to Water?," *Journal of Human Rights,* January–March 2010.

For Further Discussion

Chapter 1

1. The concept of the universality of human rights has often caused debate. Some Islamic countries, for example, reject the UN Universal Declaration of Human Rights because they claim it defines specific rights from a Western perspective that does not respect Muslim law or values. Stephen Kinzer warns in his viewpoint that human rights activists need to be aware that countries define rights uniquely based on religious, political, and cultural need. Do you believe Kinzer's argument is valid? Is it appropriate for the United Nations or any international body to define universal rights and expect nations to adhere to them? Explain your answer by referring to Kinzer and Dipo Djungdjungan Summa's articles.

2. Li Guowen outlines the steps that China's government claims it is taking to enhance the rights of its citizens while also participating in the promotion of human rights around the globe. Based on Guowen's viewpoint and the assessment by Amnesty International, do you think China is making fair progress in reforming its poor human rights reputation? Who should be the judge of this progress?

3. Lila Abu-Lughod insists that the West has mischaracterized Middle Eastern women as oppressed victims in need of rescue because of their dress and their obedience to community values. She believes women of the region have demonstrated their power for reform while maintaining customs that are important to them. Is Abu-Lughod's argument convincing? Why would the United States and other Western nations want to portray Middle Eastern women as victims? Explain your views using evidence from her viewpoint as well as Sanja Kelly's viewpoint.

Chapter 2

1. After reading the first two viewpoints in this chapter, decide whether you think the United States should join the International Criminal Court. Do you believe, like Butch Bracknell, that the United States is compromising its commitment to global justice by refraining from joining, or do you agree with Brett Schaefer and Steven Groves that the United States cannot afford to sacrifice jurisdiction over its citizens? Explain your answer using quotes from the viewpoints.

2. Research two rights that the LGBT community in the United States has fought for, and then describe the current status of those rights. Does the progress made on those rights seem to support Hillary Rodham Clinton's positive assessment of the Barack Obama administration's commitment to LGBT rights? That is, is it fair to tout the United States as a global leader in promoting LGBT rights?

Chapter 3

1. Eric Schulzke offers numerous examples of situations in which the right to religious freedom is being threatened. Miklos Haraszti argues to the contrary that religious freedom is being used as an excuse to limit other human rights, particularly free speech. Conduct research about current events regarding these issues worldwide. In light of your findings, do you believe religious freedom or freedom of speech is under greater threat? How are the two related, if at all? Use examples to make your argument and expand on the points made by either Schulzke or Haraszti.

2. Austin Dacey and Colin Koproske emphasize what they see as the fundamental disconnect between Islamic formulations of human rights and those generally accepted by the United Nations and the West, while Asma T. Uddin maintains that the gap between the two is based on a misunderstanding,

not irreconcilable differences. With which viewpoint do you agree more? Does the background of the authors influence your trust in their opinion? Use examples from the viewpoints to support your claims.

3. In examining the influence of the Catholic Church on reproductive rights, Nancy Northup focuses on both US and global examples of instances where the Church has, in her view, infringed upon women's rights. John Garvey instead focuses just on the United States and how new health-care laws regarding provision of care will, in his view, violate freedom of religion. How do you think Northup's international examples compare with Garvey's US example? Does cultural context change your belief regarding this situation? Why? Cite the viewpoints in your answer to back up your argument.

Chapter 4

1. Much of the debate surrounding the right to water centers on whether water should be considered a public good or a commodity. Maude Barlow believes the former, arguing that because it is necessary to life, water must be readily available to all humans. Conduct additional research into the perceived differences between public versus private control of goods and services. Do you believe that making water a public good or a commodity will make it more accessible?

2. When arguing about whether Internet access can be considered a human right, JD Rucker and Vinton G. Cerf disagree about whether a tool that enables individuals to realize their human rights can be considered a right in itself. Find outside articles discussing the use of the Internet in the recent democratic uprisings in the Middle East. Do you believe these uprisings would have been possible without the Internet? Did Internet access enable these individuals to fight more effectively for their human rights? Would lack of

access infringe upon their ability to freely express and gather to protest their governments? Use specific examples from the viewpoints and your research in your answer.

3. The articles in this chapter debate whether certain rights can be considered human rights. After reading these viewpoints, find the Universal Declaration of Human Rights (UDHR) online. Are there any rights not included in this document that you believe should be considered human rights? What are they, and why do you think they should be included in the UDHR? Conversely, are there any rights that you see in the UDHR that you believe do not warrant protection under this declaration? Explain why.

Organizations to Contact

The editors have compiled the following list of organizations concerned with the issues debated in this book. The descriptions are derived from materials provided by the organizations. All have publications or information available for interested readers. The list was compiled on the date of publication of the present volume; the information provided here may change. Be aware that many organizations take several weeks or longer to respond to inquiries, so allow as much time as possible.

American Civil Liberties Union (ACLU)
125 Broad Street, 18th Floor
New York, NY 10004
(212) 607-3300 • fax: (212) 607-3318
website: www.aclu.org

The ACLU seeks to ensure that all Americans are afforded the same civil liberties as guaranteed by the US Constitution by providing aid to individuals, such as minorities, women, lesbians, gay men, bisexuals, and transgender (LGBT) people, who have historically been deprived of their rights. While the ACLU focuses mainly on civil rights, its work is closely related to human rights because Constitutional rights often intersect with human rights. Publications concerning free speech, religious freedom, LGBT rights, and women's rights can all be accessed on the ACLU website.

American Enterprise Institute (AEI)
1150 Seventeenth Street NW
Washington, DC 20036
(202) 862-5800 • fax: (202) 862-7177
website: www.aei.org

AEI is a public policy think tank that analyzes US government policy, publishes a range of materials containing policy suggestions, and holds conferences to foster debate on policy issues. AEI offers a range of publications analyzing the status of human rights observance both in the United States and worldwide and proposing positions the US government should take to advance human rights. Articles such as "Time to Pressure China on Human Rights" and "Don't Sacrifice Human Rights for Iran Diplomacy" as well as testimony and commentary on the United States' role in the UN Human Rights Commission and the International Criminal Court can be accessed on the AEI website.

Amnesty International
5 Penn Plaza, 16th Floor
New York, NY 10001
(212) 807-8400 • fax: (212) 463-9193
e-mail: admin-us@aiusa.org
website: www.amnesty.org

Amnesty International is a non-governmental organization that works on a global level to ensure that every individual on the planet has the same human rights as defined by international standards and the Universal Declaration of Human Rights. With members in more than 150 countries worldwide, Amnesty International works locally to correct the most egregious human rights abuses being committed within specific regions. The organization's work covers human rights ranging from discrimination to arms control and economic, social, and cultural rights. The Amnesty International website provides detailed information about the status of human rights worldwide.

Blue Planet Project
c/o The Council of Canadians
170 Laurier Avenue West
Ottawa, ON K1P 5V5
(613) 233-2773; (800) 387-7177
website: www.blueplanetproject.net

The Blue Planet Project is an international civil society movement launched by the Council for Canadians to mitigate the negative effects of trade and privatization on water access. Working within a human rights framework, the project partners with grassroots activists who work on the local level to defend community controlled water and coordinates with international organizations to establish a UN treaty guaranteeing the right to water. The Blue Planet Project website defines the human right to water and offers numerous publications detailing the basis for this right.

Cato Institute
1000 Massachusetts Avenue NW
Washington, DC 20001-5403
(202) 842-0200 • fax: (202) 842-3490
website: www.cato.org

Cato is a libertarian organization dedicated to promoting the principles of limited government, individual liberty, free markets, and peace. While human rights in itself is not a dedicated research area of the institute, Cato explores the impact of human rights on numerous other issues including trade, development, and globalization. Articles such as "Wrong about Human Rights," "Human Rights, Limited Government, and Capitalism," and "Globalization, Human Rights, and Democracy" can be accessed on the Cato website.

Center for American Progress (CAP)
1333 H Street NW, 10th Floor
Washington, DC 20005
(202) 682-1611 • fax: (202) 682-1867
website: www.americanprogress.org

CAP is a progressive public policy think tank that seeks to advance the lives of Americans by challenging conservative-based policy and media coverage. While the work of the organization focuses mainly on the United States, the organization's publications have explored the country's role in domestic and foreign human rights issues. Articles such as "Congress Deserves a Voice on Human Rights in Russia," "Domestic Human Rights and National Security," and "Reproductive Rights Are Human Rights: A Global Perspective" can be accessed on the CAP website.

Center for Reproductive Rights

120 Wall Street
New York, NY 10005
(917) 637-3600 • fax (917) 637-3666
e-mail: info@reprorights.org
website: www.reproductiverights.org

The Center for Reproductive Rights employs a legal framework as it seeks to advance reproductive freedom as a human right guaranteed by both the US Constitution and the Universal Declaration of Human Rights. The center sees reproductive freedom as necessary to women's equal participation and membership in society. Areas of focus include abortion, contraception, and HIV/AIDS. Publications such as "Reproductive Rights Violations as Torture" and "Abortion Worldwide: Seventeen Years of Reform" can be read on the center's website.

Global Policy Forum (GPF)

777 UN Plaza, Suite 3D
New York, NY 10017
(212) 557-3161 • fax: (212) 557-3165
e-mail: gpf@globalpolicy.org
website: www.globalpolicy.org

GPF was founded in 1993 to serve as a watchdog over the United Nations and analyze its global policymaking decisions. Human rights play a crucial role in much of the organization's work, particularly with regard to international justice, world food and hunger, and humanitarian intervention. Articles about the organization's current work in these areas and others can be accessed on the GPF website.

Heritage Foundation

214 Massachusetts Avenue NE
Washington, DC 20002-4999
(202) 546-4400 • fax: (202) 546-8328
e-mail: info@heritage.org
website: www.heritage.org

The Heritage Foundation is a conservative public policy organization espousing the ideals of free enterprise, limited government, individual freedom, traditional US values, and a strong national defense. Heritage scholars examine the status of human rights worldwide and assess US engagement on these issues, suggesting future policy directions and initiatives. Articles published by the foundation promote limited US involvement in international bodies such as the United Nations and the International Criminal Court but advocate for a strong US leadership position as essential to securing freedom and democracy worldwide. The Heritage website provides access to reports such as "Understanding America" and "The UN Human Rights Council: No Better for Obama's Engagement."

Human Rights Watch (HRW)

350 Fifth Avenue, 34th Floor
New York, NY 10118-3299
(212) 290-4700
website: www.hrw.org

HRW is an international organization that defends and protects human rights worldwide. Since 1978, HRW has worked to investigate human rights abuses, present detailed information about these cases, and utilize the media to raise awareness about human rights transgressions around the world. The organization's work spans the range of human rights and can be searched by topic or region on its website.

International Criminal Court (ICC)

PO Box 19519
2500 CM The Hague
The Netherlands
31 (0)70 515-8515 • fax: 31 (0)70 515-8555
website: www.icc-cpi.int

The ICC is an international, treaty-based criminal court created with the goal of holding perpetrators accountable for the crimes they commit. The court prosecutes only those who have allegedly committed grave crimes such as genocide, crimes against humanity, and war crimes, and only when national proceedings fail to provide justice for those impacted by these crimes. Information about the specific crimes the court has tried can be found on the ICC website along with annual reports on the court's activities.

International Gay and Lesbian Human Rights Commission (IGLHRC)

80 Maiden Lane, Suite 1505
New York, NY 10038
(212) 430-6054 • fax (212) 430-6060
e-mail: iglhrc@iglhrc.org
website: www.iglhrc.org

IGLHRC is an international organization dedicated to protecting the human rights of individuals subjected to discrimination as a result of their sexual orientation or gender identity. Its work focuses on four main areas: eradicating laws, policies, and practices that sanction discrimination; promoting laws, policies, and practices that fight discrimination; limiting the incidence of violence against LGBT individuals; and furthering economic, social, and cultural rights for all regardless of their sexual orientation or gender identity. Information about specific issues and campaigns by country can be accessed on the IGLHRC website.

United Nations (UN)
140 East 45th Street
New York, NY 10017
(212) 415-4000 • fax: (212) 415-4443
e-mail: usa@un.int
website: www.un.org

In 1948, the UN established an international definition of human rights with the signing of the Universal Declaration of Human Rights. Since then, this international alliance of membership organizations has sought to ensure that human rights are upheld around the world. The Office of the High Commissioner for Human Rights is specifically charged with guaranteeing human rights worldwide, and this office's website provides detailed information about human rights issues and international law, regional human rights programs, and access to a range of publications about specific human rights topics.

US Agency for International Development (USAID)
Information Center
Ronald Reagan Building
Washington, DC 20523-1000
(202) 712-4810 • fax: (202) 216-3524
website: www.usaid.gov

Since its founding in 1961, USAID has been the agency charged with allocating federal assistance to countries worldwide with the dual goals of advancing US interests and helping citizens of developing countries improve their lives. Most USAID programs focus on fostering economic growth, agriculture and trade, global health, democracy, or a combination of these. Details about ongoing and past USAID initiatives, including Feed the Future, Global Climate Change, and The Global Health Initiative, can be found on the agency's website.

Bibliography of Books

Michael N. Barnett   *Empire of Humanity: A History
of Humanitarianism.* Ithaca, NY:
Cornell University Press, 2011.

Charles Beitz   *The Idea of Human Rights.* New
York: Oxford University Press,
2009.

Frank Ching   *China: The Truth About Its
Human Rights Record.* London:
Rider, 2008.

Noam Chomsky   *The Umbrella of US Power: The
Universal Declaration of Human
Rights and the Contradictions
of US Policy.* New York: Seven
Stories Press, 1999.

Rosemary Foot   *Rights Beyond Borders: The Global
Community and the Struggle over
Human Rights in China.* New
York: Oxford University Press,
2000.

Jennifer Harbury   *Truth, Torture, and the
American Way: The History and
Consequences of US Involvement
in Torture.* Boston, MA: Beacon,
2005.

John M. Headley   *The Europeanization of the World:
On the Origins of Human Rights
and Democracy.* Princeton, NJ:
Princeton University Press, 2008.

David Hollenbach

The Global Face of Public Faith: Politics, Human Rights, and Christian Ethics. Washington, DC: Georgetown University Press, 2003.

Shale Horowitz and Albrecht Schnabel, eds.

Human Rights and Societies in Transition: Causes, Consequences, Responses. New York: United Nations University Press, 2004.

Lynn Avery Hunt

Inventing Human Rights: A History. New York: W.W. Norton & Co., 2007.

Micheline R. Ishay, ed.

The Human Rights Reader: Major Political Essays, Speeches, and Documents from Ancient Times to the Present, second ed. New York: Routledge, 2007.

Sanja Kelly and Julia Breslin, eds.

Women's Rights in the Middle East and North Africa: Progress Amid Resistance. New York: Freedom House, 2010.

George Kent

Freedom from Want: The Human Right to Adequate Food. Washington, DC: Georgetown University Press, 2005.

Paul Gordon Lauren

The Evolution of International Human Rights: Visions Seen, third ed. Philadelphia: University of Pennsylvania Press, 2011.

Ann Elizabeth Mayer

Islam and Human Rights: Tradition and Politics, fourth ed. Boulder, CO: Westview Press, 2007.

Shadi Mokhtari	*After Abu Ghraib: Exploring Human Rights in America and the Middle East.* New York: Cambridge University Press, 2009.
Joel Peters	*The European Union and the Arab Spring: Promoting Democracy and Human Rights in the Middle East.* Lanham, MD: Lexington Books, 2012.
Helle Porsdam	*Civil Religion, Human Rights and International Relations: Connecting People Across Cultures and Traditions.* Northampton, MA: Edward Elgar, 2012.
Kathreyn Sikkink	*The Justice Cascade: How Human Rights Prosecutions Are Changing World Politics.* New York: W.W. Norton & Co., 2011.
Farhana Sultana and Alex Loftus, eds.	*The Right to Water: Politics, Governance and Social Struggles.* New York: Earthscan/Routledge, 2012.
Aurora Voiculescu and Helen Yanacopulos, eds.	*The Business of Human Rights: An Evolving Agenda for Corporate Responsibility.* New York: Zed Books, 2011.
John Witte, Jr. and M. Christian Green, eds.	*Religion and Human Rights: An Introduction.* New York: Oxford University Press, 2012.
Minky Worden, ed.	*The Unfinished Revolution: Voices from the Global Fight for Women's Rights.* New York: Seven Stories Press, 2012.

Index

CPSIA information can be obtained
at www.ICGtesting.com
Printed in the USA
FFOW030557050213
825FF